CLOSED DOORS

AN ANSWER TO *BITTER LEMONS* BY LAWRENCE DURRELL

Costas Montis (1914-2004)

COSTAS MONTIS

Closed Doors

An Answer to *Bitter Lemons*
by Lawrence Durrell

TRANSLATED FROM GREEK BY

DAVID ROESSEL

AND

SOTERIOS G. STAVROU

WITH AN INTRODUCTION BY

DAVID ROESSEL

A NOSTOS BOOK
2004

This volume is number twenty-three in a series of publications dealing with modern Greek history and culture, under the auspices of Nostos, the Society for the Study of Greek Life and Thought, Minneapolis, Minnesota, and in collaboration with the Modern Greek Studies Program at the University of Minnesota.

Theofanis G. Stavrou, *general editor*

Cover and frontispiece: Photo of Costas Montis (1914-2004)

Technical and editorial assistance for this volume was provided by Elizabeth Harry.

δώρων δ', ὅσσ' ἐν ἐμῷ οἴκῳ κειμήλια κεῖται,
δώσω ὃ κάλλιστον καὶ τιμηέστατόν ἐστι.

Homer

ACKNOWLEDGEMENTS

I FIRST READ Costas Montis's "answer to *Bitter Lemons* of Lawrence Durrell" when I was in Athens in 1993 at the urging of Garo Yacopian. The following year I met Mr. Montis in Nicosia and asked why there had been no attempt to translate the book into English. He handed me a typescript of a translation done in the late sixties or early seventies by a young Cypriot who was killed in the Turkish invasion of 1974. The translator's name did not appear on the typescript and, try as he might, Mr. Montis could not recall it after twenty years. When he asked me to peruse it to see if it could be used, I could hardly refuse. But the version was not, unfortunately, ready for publication in English, and attempts to fix it caused a clash of styles that only seemed to mar the text further. Over the next two years, I encouraged several people to try their hand at a new translation of the book, but all were too busy to undertake the job. In 1996, Dr. Nancy Serwint, the director of the Cyprus Archaeological Research Institute (CAARI), and Gerald L. Vincent, a former acting director of the same institution, suggested I stop talking about the need for a translation of *Closed Doors* and do something about it. When as a fellow of CAARI in 1998 I worked on the translation of this story about the Cypriot struggle against the British in the 1950s, I felt over my shoulder the presence of the first translator, whose name I have never known and would provide if I knew it.

I sent a draft of the completed translation to Theofanis Stavrou of the University of Minnesota and the general editor of Nostos Press, a publisher known for their commitment to translations of modern Cypriot writers. Theofanis passed it on to his brother Soterios for comment. The diligence and self-lessness with which he made my text his text has been a model for cooperative endeavor, and it was only fair that I insisted that we add Soterios's name to the title page.

This book would not exist without the kind of support that translators of works by authors from small countries rarely receive. I received a joint CAARI/NEH fellowship to work on translation in Cyprus for five months in 1998. On other occasions, I was able to visit Nicosia with the help of Yiorgos Moleskis and the Ministry of Cultural Affairs of the Republic of Cyprus, and Daniel Hadjitoffi and the Cyprus Fulbright Foundation. And finally, the Leventis Foundation stepped in at a crucial moment and generously offered a subvention to help with costs of publication.

During work on the draft in Nicosia, I spent many hours with Costas Montis and Yiorgos Phillipou Pierides, two giants both as writers and as people. The generosity of the entire Montis family continues to this day. I would also like to thank all the people in Cyprus who offered aid and support, in particular Phivos Stravrides, Dafni Charalambides and her father, poet Kyriakos Charalambides, Ruth Keshishian, Vathoulla Moustoukki, Vassilis and Diana Constantinides, Maria Stavrou, Niki Marangou, Michalis Pieris, Peter McGaw, Diane Bolger, and Maria Pieridou-Hadjikakou. After my return from Cyprus, Arnold Rampersad, Edmund Keeley, Will Howarth, Carrie Cowherd, and Nicholas Moschovakis provided continual encouragement. To Elizabeth Harry, who patiently typeset the manuscript and made many revisions and numerous suggestions, I am grateful. Finally, to Elizabeth Stavrou and Pamela Beatrice, who have read the text times beyond counting, the debt is deep and enduring.

I still remember my surprise when I received an answer to my request for funding from the Leventis Foundation —signed by Constantine Leventis himself. Constantine Leventis and the Leventis Foundation have had a long interest in the work of Costas Montis, and supported the publication of the multivolume collected works of the author. All those involved in Greek letters will miss him.

David Roessel

INTRODUCTION

by David Roessel

"AN ANSWER to *Bitter Lemons* of Lawrence Durrell." These
words on the title page of Costas Montis's *Closed Doors* provide the inspiration and the context for the novel. For, while
the book can certainly be read on a number of different levels,
it is fundamentally a dialogue in which the other side has already spoken. And an answer, even such an indirect answer as
this, does not claim to be neutral or unbiased. American readers will find in *Closed Doors* a relentless, sometimes strident,
Cypriot point of view. This is a clear case of the "empire writing back," a colonized native answering a former servant in the
colonial government. In fact, the two books share a geography
of adjoining offices. Lawrence Durrell began *Bitter Lemons*
near the end of his stint from 1954 to 1956 as the director of
the Public Information Office (PIO) for the British Colonial
Government of Cyprus; Costas Montis wrote *Closed Doors*
while the director of tourism for the Republic of Cyprus, a bu-
reau which was formerly under Durrell's control. Yet, while
Bitter Lemons (1957) has sold over two million copies, *Closed
Doors* has never appeared in English translation and readers of
Durrell are unaware of its existence. This translation finally
allows Montis's voice to be heard by those who cannot read
Greek. The dialogue between *Bitter Lemons* and *Closed Doors*
has interest beyond scholars involved in Durrell research or
postcolonial studies, for it is also a debate between two powerful artists who produced political books to influence the depiction of the narrative of the struggle for Cypriot independence.
For Montis, *Closed Doors* was an attempt to reappropriate that
narrative from Durrell, to present a picture of the struggle for

freedom by a Cypriot who, as he says in his brief explanation, had lived through the entire four years of the revolt. In a discussion of *Bitter Lemons* in a suppressed section of his novel *The Age of Bronze* (1960), the Greek author Rodis Roufos wrote that "(a)nother book was needed to fill in the gaps, to give the Greek view," because Durrell "observes a prudish silence over some aspects of the repression" (this section was published for the first time as "Sour Grapes," in *Deus Loci: The Lawrence Durrell Journal*, no. 3 [1994]: 134-38). Durrell may seem enjoyable and plausible to American readers because, as part of the English-speaking community, he knows how to frame the story to impress and influence them. Montis, writing in Greek for a Cypriot audience, employs a different style and strategy. Where Durrell wants ambiguity, Montis appears polemical—his self-perceived function is to stress the torture chambers, curfews, communal fines, and black-hooded informers that were part of daily Cypriot life during the struggle. While *Closed Doors* is a novel, it has more similarities to Zola's *J'accuse* than to the usual qualities of fiction. Further, it is important to keep in mind that Montis, like Rodis Roufos, perceived a deviousness in Durrell's supposed ambiguity. It was, in their eyes, the cloak that the colonial spin doctor used to mislead his readers. In fact, both Montis and Roufos chose to write their responses to *Bitter Lemons* in the form of fiction in part to indicate that *Bitter Lemons* was itself highly fictional.

§

What was at stake for Montis, as I mentioned earlier, was the narrative of the struggle for Cypriot freedom. Cyprus, which came under British control in 1878, acquired the status of a crown colony in 1926. The overwhelming desire of the Greek Cypriots, over 80 percent of the population, was *enosis* (union) with Greece. But a new conception of the empire had emerged after World War II, one in which British influence and control were ensured by a skeleton of strong points such as Gibraltar, Malta, Singapore, and Hong Kong. Cyprus was to be the British base in the eastern Mediterranean, and in Parliament the foreign minister informed the members that Cyprus would "never" be let go. In addition, the Turkish Cypriots, about a fifth of the population, strenuously opposed union with Greece, as did Turkey itself. The Turks held that if the

British were to leave Cyprus, the island should revert back to Turkey, from whom the British had taken it. Whether or not some solution to the ethnic disagreement could be found, it became the policy of Britain to inflame Turkish feeling in order to counter the claims of the Greek Cypriots for enosis.

After the failure of nonviolent attempts to gain self-determination, the Cypriots began an armed rebellion on 1 April 1955 similar in kind to that which had proved effective in Palestine in 1948. It lasted, with several breaks and ceasefires, until 1959. British officials bear some responsibility for this development as they thoughtlessly offered the opinion that "if the Cypriot people want Enosis, they would fight for it" (Charles Foley, *Island in Revolt* [1962], 27). The aim of the armed struggle was not to push the British off the island by force, but rather to make it too difficult and dangerous for them to stay. In the end, the strategy worked. The British offered the island independence rather than enosis in 1959, and Archbishop Makarios, the leader of the Greek Cypriots, accepted. For all Durrell's lamentation about the "terrorists" of EOKA, the National Organization of Cypriot Fighters, the truth remains that only the armed struggle forced the British to grant the Cypriots some measure of self-determination.

In *Bitter Lemons*, the armed rebellion is presented in consistently negative terms, as the work of "terrorists" who compel the populace, generally pro-British, to assist the revolt through threats of assassination. For example, Durrell said that "to the nauseating foulness of the street murder of soldiers and policemen was added the disgusting, typically Balkan, murder of civilians suspected of being traitors. Apart from this of course there was many an old score to settle in the name of Enosis. The black mask was protection enough" (217). Durrell concedes that the announcement that Cyprus would never be permitted self-determination was a mistake, and that the British made other errors of policy, but contends that they were generally humane.

The truth was that the majority of Greek Cypriots did solidly support the armed struggle—if not, why were the British so quick to impose communal penalties such as curfews and fines? And civilians had just as much to fear from the hooded informers working for the British, local "supergrasses" who could consign someone to prison and torture by simply pointing at them, as from the masked gunmen of EOKA. Both sides engaged in terror on Cyprus. Some British writers, such as Durrell's contemporary Charles Foley (in *Island in Revolt*), acknowledged this fact.

Despite Durrell's position as the chief "spin doctor" for the British on Cyprus and the publication of *Bitter Lemons* in the midst of the Cypriot struggle for independence, his book has a reputation for fairness and impartiality among English-speaking readers. Critics have been willing to believe that Durrell, despite his work in the PIO, was quite capable of writing a book without bias. For decades, amazingly, they have taken the first sentence of *Bitter Lemons* at face value: "This is not a political book, but simply a somewhat impressionistic study of the moods and atmospheres of Cyprus during the troubled years 1953-6." We quickly discover in *Bitter Lemons* that what made the years 1953 to 1956 troubled was the political situation. Durrell's book remains the most widely known volume in English about Cyprus and, in the eyes of many Cypriots, has given readers a slanted view of the island's struggle to free itself from British rule.

A number of Cypriots responded in reviews to Durrell's depiction of Cyprus, but almost everyone with any knowledge of Cypriot literature would agree that Costas Montis is the writer whom Cyprus would want as their voice in that dialogue. He is widely recognized as Cyprus's greatest poet and has been called the "voice of the island." It struck me as rather shameful that, given the status of Montis, *Closed Doors* had not appeared in English earlier.

§

Costas Montis was a leading member in what might be called "the Cypriot Renaissance," the generation which matured in the forties and fifties and laid the firm foundation for modern Cypriot literature. Montis was born in Famagusta in 1914 and died in Nicosia in 2004. He studied law at the University of Athens, but upon his return to Cyprus he never practiced as a lawyer. After a varied career as a school teacher, journalist, and editor, he served as the director of tourism from 1960 until his retirement in 1976. He helped to found the first professional theater in Cyprus in 1942 and wrote several works in the Cypriot dialect, including a number of adaptations of the plays of Aristophanes. Montis gained renown as a poet with the appearance in 1958 of *Moments*, which was followed in the next decade by his masterpiece, the long poetic sequence *Letters to Mother*. The poetry of Montis resonates with the travails of his island, from the struggle for union with Greece, the acceptance of independence, the intercommunal violence in the 1960s, the invasion of the island by Turkey in 1974, and the subsequent division of the small island into two distinct units. *Closed Doors* is one of only two novels by Montis and is not one of his best-known works. But for English and Americans it has a special interest because of its relationship to Lawrence Durrell.

§

Closed Doors is not, as Montis repeatedly stated, a direct answer to *Bitter Lemons*. He simply presents a version of the struggle by a Cypriot who lived through it. Montis's choice of a narrator may have been influenced by Durrell. One of the interesting things about *Bitter Lemons* is the way that Durrell attempts to present himself as an innocent, even naïve narrator, who is constantly surprised by events—even his own appointment as PIO director. This is, in part, a strategy to make the reader trust Durrell's narrative, although at times it stretches credulity. For example, Durrell suggests that it was only when he took the job as PIO director that he realized the importance that Turkey would have for the island's future. Surely that would have been apparent to any intelligent adult with a background in the foreign service? Why, we should wonder, would the British want someone as PIO director who could not see this? Against the innocent, childlike Durrell of *Bitter Lemons*, Montis offers a child who is just a freshman in high school at the start of his book. One of the virtues of *Closed Doors* is how it can present the unfolding movement through a set of wide and impressionable eyes. And his choice of narrator underscores one of his main themes, how a generation of Cypriot youngsters lost their childhood because the British saw Cyprus as a strategic base. Durrell would like us to think that he is a normal English civilian put at risk by the terror of EOKA; Montis, on the other hand, centers our attention on an entire generation sacrificed for British policy. Despite his announcement that his "was not a political book," Durrell talks a great deal about politics and policies. Montis, with his young narrator, dispenses with high politics and focuses on the impact of events on everyday life.

In structure, *Closed Doors* is very much a poet's book, a series of vignettes that resemble prose poems that center on one particular family but range widely. In this it resembles Montis's long verse sequences, *Moments* and *Letters to Mother*. In *Moments*, for example, Montis constructs both a perception of the world and a philosophy by means of short, epigrammatic sections of verse, often just a single sentence.

> They start us with fairy tales
> on our grandmother's knee;
> they start us with the most unfit prologue,
> with the most dangerous introduction.

> At the loom of Penelope we play,
> worse still,
> because we the lovers
> ourselves unravel the web.
> . . . .
> Who knows what signatures we forge,
> with what orbits we become entangled.
> They locked our brain into its shell,
> a captain without a bridge,
> and they fill it with what they wish.
> *(translated by Charles Dodd and Amaranth Sitas)*

The brevity and specificity of these sections led the great critic of Greek poetry G. P. Savvides to call Montis "the poet of small things." In the modernist tradition, Montis leaves the reader to find connections between the sections on his or her own, to create the whole through his or her reading. Montis employs the same strategy in *Closed Doors*. We are not told why, near the end of the book, the text seems to break for an apostrophe to a soldier from Ireland killed in Cyprus. It is, Montis would say, a thread in the story, and it is up to us as readers to understand how such threads are sewn together. The poet can only take us so far.

§

Closed Doors is also a careful record of Nicosia during the emergency measures under the British in the 1950s. In the

Leventis Museum in Nicosia, I saw a video called "School Memories," which contained footage of students confronting riot police in the city in the fifties. I stood mesmerized, for it was as though I was watching an adaptation of a section of *Closed Doors*—that was how accurately Montis has depicted the collision between students and police. The scenes when the British closed the walls of the old cities, the flying of kites from rooftops during the long curfews, the "language war" in which English signs were painted over, all of these are accurate depictions of what life had been like and bring nods of agreement from older residents of the city.

§

The metaphor of closed doors forms a crucial part of the mental territory of Montis's universe, and we can begin to see the key place of the image in Montis's thought only after reading this novel. And since the poet is a spokesman for his society and for Cyprus, we can understand how closed doors function as a metaphor for the Cypriot experience. The doors in the title refer on one level to the doors of the prisons and camps which were opened in 1959—an incident captured in the monument of liberty near the Famagusta Gate in Nicosia—as well as the many sorts of doors which were never opened upon independence. It also refers to the lack of communication—between Durrell's book and the Cypriots in particular and between people more generally. Montis returns to the image of closed doors over and over again, as in the following passages:

> The strange thing is that while there were so many open doors
> We were always guided to the closed doors,
> The strange thing is that while there so many open doors,
> We always fixed ourselves outside of the closed doors,
> We relied on the closed doors,
> We took our chances with the closed doors.

> In every circumstance, weeping will close the door at last.

> Consider that there is no other dream for us except to exit by the door.

Let the door finally close,
Let the windows finally close,
Let those alleged openings to the street finally close.

The theme is also central to the poem, "Before the Curfew":

"Before the Curfew"
We still have an hour at our disposal,
Before the curfew closes us within the house.
We will run here and there,
We will do one thing or another,
Whatever we have time for.
This time-limit pleases us,
This deadline excites us strangely
And we have to agree
That, curiously without displeasure,
We will hand ourselves over at six
And we will enter the house and close the door.

We as readers must keep one essential fact in mind. For Durrell, the lemons of Cyprus were bitter for a few years; for Montis, some of the doors closed by colonialism are still closed. Durrell and the British could walk away from the intractable problem that they helped to create on Cyprus; in fact, Durrell never visited the island again. For Montis, the bitter lemons and closed doors remain part of daily life on the divided island. If Montis's book seems too angry and polemical, it is because both he and his island are still living with the legacy of the colonial government that Durrell served. It may be that we in the West will have to learn how to read "answers" that re-appropriate a colonial narrative before we can truly appreciate them. *Closed Doors* is, as Montis admits, an annoying and frustrating book, but it is also intriguing and eye-opening. It deserves a place on the shelf.

AN EXPLANATION

MY LAST COLLECTION of stories (*Humble Life*) appeared in 1944. Since then I have not concertedly focused on writing fiction. A life of trials, worries, and disappointments shattered my sense of continuity. So, on the few occasions when the pen rebelled and seized my hand, I turned to poetry, an elliptical poetry, which shared its chats with the silence. My drawers remained as I left them twenty years earlier—full of half-finished stories, sketches, beginnings, and titles. Until suddenly the Revolution came to take control and concentrate my fragmented thoughts (on the spur of the moment—yes, just like that if you will). Until it came to the point that there was no escaping the fact that someone had to speak out, someone who had lived through those remarkable four years.

I do not know the degree to which the many parentheses that I use will surprise and annoy. I first employed the parentheses in 1944 for the stories in *Humble Life*, and as I began to write twenty years later, there they were, stubbornly waiting for me. I could not find any other way to juxtapose the complete picture with the steps that led up to it, to include the doubts that question it, the small things that give it significance, and the lacunae that are not explained, unless I wrote simultaneously on two or three planes. As there is no doubt that the subject has to be dealt with at some length, and it has to be soon, some means must be found to tell it. We can no longer merely observe life, eternally utilizing the same white paper and pencil.

CLOSED DOORS

WHEN IN 1955 the Revolution began in Cyprus, and the small Mediterranean island unexpectedly rose up to rid itself of English rule, the three of us were students in high school—I a freshman, my sister Stalo a sophomore, and my brother Nikos a junior—three closely successive steps in our parents' affection.

We lived in Ayios Dometios, a suburb of Nicosia, which, due to its proximity to the airport, had seen the largest share of the city's sudden growth over the previous few years. No one had foreseen the rapid expansion and consequent complications of unfettered development.

Our father had a good position, but we just managed to make ends meet even though we owned our home, a significant consideration in a time of uncontrolled escalation in rents, especially in our suburb that had experienced the greatest influx of English families.

I was leading the carefree life of a fifteen-year-old, with its romantic outlook, its deepening of the voice, its stirrings of new desires, and its joys and sorrows.

As for the political agitation and the long-standing struggle of the island to shake off the foreign yoke, an unbroken effort that had taken many forms, all peaceful (how could it have been otherwise, you might ask, when such a powerful empire controlled us?), we children (really, when does childhood begin and end?) accepted the mild level of protest as customary, traditional even. It had been closely interwoven into our lives since birth. Until that fateful (fateful?) January, the desire for union with Greece, Enosis, flowed in a consistent, predictable stream without floods or tidal waves, almost unnoticed and unremarkable. Once or twice a year we would get up at four in the morning in order to sing hymns and other songs first in the cobblestone square in front of the

3

Archbishop's Palace and then in front of the Consulate (for us there was only one consulate—the Greek). Then we marched with Greek flags to the rhythm of drums and the blare of trumpets, the music beating upon our fifteen years and resounding within us. We were elated that our parents and all our neighbors lined the streets to watch us go by. Finally, everyone would squeeze together inside the Phaneromeni Cathedral to cry for "Enosis," a demand for liberation that echoed from time to time as the ultimate aspiration of every Greek territory outside of the borders of the free motherland. In school, we wrote enthusiastic essays about freedom and we drew large, neat, straight-lined blue and white Greek flags. Our breasts swelled with an odd emotion when we heard speeches about Greece, like when you want to cry but struggle to control yourself (I don't know how to describe the feeling exactly: a kind of crying without tears?). Still, as I said, familiarity had so reduced our idea of Enosis that it did not really disturb us, at least it did not disturb us continually or urgently dominate our thoughts. It did not look us straight in the eye; it did not follow us in the streets, at home, in bed. It did not spring up suddenly from our books and grab our hands, causing our pencils to fall (I think I've said enough about school for the moment).

A collective memory of the October Uprising of 1931 still existed in us, but I don't know why after so short a time (only twenty years) it seemed so lifeless and uninspiring. For example, we listened greedily ("listening greedily" really has no meaning for children, other factors often come into play), greedily, yet at the same time coldly (do you suspect now an inconsistency in each phrase? very well, then, expect an inconsistency), as our father related how, as a senior in high school, he had taken part in the riots in '31 and had been in the middle of the crowd that had surrounded and set fire to the Government House. How, at a moment's notice, the principal of the school had assigned him the task of eulogizing the first casualty, "a small barefoot boy like Gavrias," he told us. How he had stayed by himself in the schoolyard to construct the words of a brief lament (as short as was possible in the circumstances) and a strong exhortation (as strong as was possible given the setting) while all of Nicosia poured inside the Phaneromeni Cathedral and into the streets nearby, or hung in clusters around the balconies and kiosks. And he felt alone, completely alone, not just in the courtyard of the school, not just in Nicosia, but alone in the whole world (there is an immense isolation when one loses touch with the universe outside oneself). A dead boy drenched in blood was waiting. (It's ridiculous how we wait upon the funeral, and cling to the speeches and flowers, as if they meant something to us, as if they had something to offer us.) He told us how he had to run breathlessly into the church just in time to deliver his oration ("Dearly departed, the Pancyprian Gymnasium kneels reverently . . .").

Greedily, but still somehow impassively, we listened as he told us about the repressive measures of the English that followed. Greek flags were banned. They completely disappeared from the streets. The people longed to see one and gathered outside the Consulate in order to behold and admire the beloved piece of cloth ("Shall we pass by the Consulate?"). Many made a wide detour on their way to work in the morning in order to walk by the Consulate, just as the shopkeepers of Nicosia, before opening their stores on Monday mornings, passed by the church to light a candle for a good week (serious, silent, morose, sniffling with a foot still in the Sunday just past, with their hats forgotten in the Sunday just past).

"Let them try and pull that flag down," they would say (they said it exactly like children. When did we say childhood begins and ends?).

The Consulate, in order to fill the huge void in their lives, each day hoisted a huge flag with a gold fringe to wave over all of Nicosia, to sing over the whole island, to mingle with the sky, to flutter in the wind unrestricted and unfettered. Old men, my father said, cried when they saw it, and the old women made the sign of the cross. That was a real flag. Now that they are everywhere again, the flags have lost some of their beauty.

All of this was related to us by my father with deep emotion, but, as I said earlier, we children did not find it especially marvelous. I can't say exactly why, perhaps because the "disturbances" of '31 had a humiliating result, perhaps because the effort was so brief, or because the people did not take up arms. Maybe (if I may pursue the question a bit further) this very indifference, this attitude that the days of '31 were simply ancient history to us, was actually a good omen for the imminent rebellion ("Ancient history." You smile with a touch of condescension at that). But it may be very important that we children, when my father spoke of his memories of '31, had also smiled with a touch of condescension.

That January (did I call it that fateful January?), everything suddenly changed, as if things had been silently building up for years, centuries even, so that the island was a powder keg ready for a match. (I wonder if we can now look back and see the "links" and "threads" with the past.) The news spread like lightning (faster than any lightning bolt) from one end of the island to the other, when a Greek caique, the *Saint George*, had been seized in some secluded bay in Paphos while unloading a shipment of arms and explosives.

Arms? (Arms?) What was this word that echoed (exploded really) upon our slumbering servitude after so many years? (You others simply can't imagine it. All of your antiwar literature cannot stand in the balance against this one shipment of arms. You think this is unfortunate? All right, it is unfortunate.) In an inconceivable moment we saw before us once again the Greek Revolution, no longer in lifeless print with beautiful, colored pictures, but alive, raw, and fierce—thundering with the force of the eyebrows of General Kolokotronis (thick as a cloud, as we drew them as children), thundering with the power of the broken sword of the warrior Dhiakos (so clumsily, subconsciously enormous), as we sketched it in our exercise books, resounding with glorious names from the past like the Inn of Gravia, Missolonghi, and Maniaki. It seemed that the horses whinnied, that the cutlasses flashed, that the air filled with battle cries from an earlier century. It was the fastest (fast? it took but the blink of a second), the most breathtaking repetition of history one could possibly imagine.

"Will we have all these things too?" (You ask, and you avert your eyes and shift your focus. How and where can you even consider this? Can you even take it in? Is there anyone who could even supply an answer? Can you stay sane even thinking about it?) Our hearts burned with agitation, our imagination was captivated by the magical word (Arms? Yes, arms!). And when we returned our gaze to the present and our immediate surroundings, we saw our schoolwork as small and insignificant, our desks as foreign toys thousands of miles away. (Does school matter now? The question is raised, at the least.) The *Saint George*, with its anchors clanking quite audibly, moored itself in our thoughts, above all other desires and dreams. No, the boat was not moored, it opened its huge white sails and took us with it, stripped free from the past, from memory, from our familial bonds ("Yes, we will go with you wherever you want"). But I am in error, it was no longer a caique, it was Saint George himself astride his white horse, more beautiful than in the icons, more erect and invincible than in the icons. We placed our hearts on the ground for him to step on with his gold sandal when he dismounted, we offered our hearts for him to step on when he mounted again, just as if our hearts were the large stone at the monastery of Skala that, it was said, he used for this purpose every Saturday night (no other foot could match that strange, twisted footprint in the rock still visited by pilgrims). And when the saint left, the clatter of the hooves of his horse on the paving stones terrified the monks, who knelt to make the sign of the cross whenever they heard it. The saint left with the candles that the girls had brought for him during the afternoon, and the jasmine, and the secrets they had whispered to him under the large ornate arch beside the church. He went, they say, to seek out the places where he first embraced Christ, the places where he shed his golden hair.

AMONG THE GROWN-UPS, to be sure, there were some with doubts. They discussed them in houses, in the streets, everywhere. Arms on Cyprus? (Yes, arms on Cyprus, the others said.) Who brought them? Had we men to take up arms? (Of course we did.) And what would we be able to do? Would we be a match for the English? (Why not?) Just a tiny bit of an island, a handful of men, half of a handful if you want. These grown-ups had been awakened a bit too early and were cranky. They later became the best of us. (Who said just a small bit of an island, who said just a handful of men?)

For many days, weeks even, the only thing that people spoke about was the caique and the arms, although there were no new developments. (Shall I suggest that the incident was left hanging in mid-air like the model caique in front of the icon of the Virgin at Kykko monastery?) The newspapers were full of articles and photographs in the beginning, and continually sought some new fact to offer the public, who devoured it and wanted more. We children, more eager than the others to receive information without any reservations, without any hesitation, read greedily indeed. Recalling the ancient stories from the haze of early childhood, we discussed and analyzed the present situation among ourselves (with halting words, changing voices, different expressions, even new ways of seeing?). We pondered those stories sitting alone in our beds, the room half dark, for many hours (do you hear the chirrup of the cricket in the corner?) before exhaustion was finally able to close our wide-awake eyes, eyes that stared at the ceiling as if they pierced through it. (What ceiling could enclose such wide-awake eyes?)

The captain of the caique, Koutalianos, occupied the largest part of our thoughts and daydreams. Not simply because he was a captain (children like captains, maybe the word "captain" carries with it a whole repertoire of stories). Nor because in the photographs in the newspapers he was a handsome seaman and, further, that we land-based islanders, a bit of anomaly I admit, but we were land-based islanders, had an innate attraction to the sea and its men. (However much we distanced ourselves from the sea, however much we weaned ourselves from it, it still drew us to it. What had we done to it, or what had it done to us?) Not only because he looked so fearlessly and contemptuously, and what a proud contempt it was, at the English who were guarding him. But also because he shared (think of the coincidence) his name with a legendary hero of our island whose deeds our grandmothers had told to us in their stories. These stories took something from the north wind that whistled outside, something from the embers of the stove, and something from the cherished memories and lost dreams of a generation past (can't you see the eyes shining as they talk?), old stories that change into ghosts and defy the sun, defy time, defy even the rationality of the adult mind. In some of the half-deserted houses where the young have left one by one and only the old folks now remain, and in some of the old barbershops of the villages, a picture of the earlier Koutalianos might still be found alongside clumsily colored lithographs of the Balkan Wars ("Evzones in Kilkis," "The conquest of Bizani," "Commander-in-Chief Constantine and Eleftherios Venizelos, Creators of Greater Greece," "Glory crowns Greeks arms"). I saw such a photograph in a mountain village of the Troodos range where we spent the summer— Koutalianos in thin, short trousers, with his feet apart and his arms stretched forward to show off his powerful, bulging muscles. On his chest were three rows of medals, and beside him a small table loaded with cups and shields. Around the edges ran a narrow strip of faded, blue velvet embroidered with daisies. The photograph was stuck in the lower right-hand corner of a mirror with a thick, ornate gold frame.

When, after the capture of the captain, we remembered (and we recalled him instantly) our grandmother's Koutalianos, we began to attribute to him all of the deeds and legends of all the heroes of the island. If before it had been Kyrioudhi, now it was Koutalianos who ripped up an entire tree to use as a pointer to ask directions ("Did you say this way or that way?"). It was Koutalianos who had lifted the column supporting the house and placed the clothes of the Turkish pasha underneath it. It was Koutalianos that . . . Koutalianos did it all now!

About the captain of the *Saint George* we heard and repeated, with our own embellishments, another set of stories. These were not formed through the whistling of the north wind, the passing of the years, or our grandmother's necessity, for she had to find something to tell us on winter nights when we pressed her to continue. ("That is the end, children." "No, it can't be finished. Tell us more.") The tales of the captain flashed suddenly from every direction. They did not wait for time or a grandmother's need, for them the heart condensed centuries into a moment, for them a mixture of several strands within a child's heart sufficed. One such story of the captain said that when the British seized him and put a pistol to his breast, he told them calmly:

"Those old pistols you point at us. In Greece we eat them for breakfast."

(You hear this and shudder. The words break the narration and make one gasp for breath.)

WHEN THE JUDICIAL INQUIRY began against the crew of the *Saint George* and their three Cypriot accomplices (the caique, for us children, was still hanging in mid-air, and curiously, we were not anxious to get on with the sequence of events, you might say that it was as if we needed the beginning of things to sink into our hearts), every evening our father would read them aloud at home so that we children could listen. Of course, we had already read the accounts of the trial several times, and he knew it.

"I know you have read the proceedings of the trial, but I will read them again."

"Yes, because we have not read them carefully," we lied in order not to deprive him of this pleasure.

"And your homework?"

"All done," we lied again.

And as he read he cried, for the umpteenth time, when one day the papers reported that Koutalianos's lawyer had produced a commendation for "meritorious conduct and bravery" from the British Commander-in-Chief of the Middle East in the Second World War. The commendation mentioned his "extremely dangerous" trips into enemy-occupied Greek waters to rescue British, Australians, and New Zealanders stranded along the coasts. When one looks back upon my father's tears from a mature vantage point, one sees how naive they were, because they flowed from the certainty that, confronted by the commendation, the Ally would remember that earlier and ultimate sacrifice, honor those unbreakable ties forged in war, and open up their arms to the captain. And instead he is being put on trial. Unbelievable!

"Now you'll see, we have produced the commendation," said my father through his tears. "We kept that bit of evidence for the very end."

Our father was not the only innocent on this score, by no means. All of Cyprus, all of Greece believed in the efficacious power of the captain's past service. Can't you remember what their ministers had said, what their papers had written? And Greece aside, what had we fought for, what had they promised us to make us join the fight?

Along with father, Cyprus, and Greece, we cried and all of us were alike in our naive trust (father, mother, all of the Greeks were just like children).

Our father would then turn the newspaper so we could see the photographs, although he knew that we had already seen them several times ("Yes, Father, please show them to us, we did not look at them carefully yet"). And with a special emotion he would point out the Consul (I have already said that for us there was only one consulate) "entering the court to observe the progress of the inquiry."

How nobly the Consul "parts" the crowd (yes, that is the word, "parts"), we exclaimed proudly. "Ah, do you think that Greece will let them get away with it? They don't know Greece very well, I tell you, they just don't know Greece at all." (What a passion we had for this consul, however customary and conventional a part of our lives he became when we marched by him on the 25th of March or on the 28th of October. It was as if we were parading before our very dreams, our fathers' dreams, our grandfathers' dreams, the dreams of the land and the sea, of the dawn and the night, of the mountains and plains of the beloved island.)

Yet there was something (and this is significant) that gnawed at us, at least us children, even more than the fate of the accused men, a concern (even if we did not rush, as I said, the sequence of events lest we lose it) that the *Saint George* had been captured unloading its very first cargo of arms. In conversations, we children told ourselves: "See here, who knows how many times it came and went?" Still, doubts existed. Was it the first and only time? We banished the idea, we looked away until we thought it had passed. But it would not leave us. If it was the first and only shipment, what then? What if the word "arms" had echoed in vain, exploded in vain, upon our servitude? Was it an empty word, a vain hope? This has importance because it shows, beyond other things (how could it have been possible to be otherwise?) how ready we were to embrace the struggle before it began. An unexpected militant maturity had evolved within us without any prior experience or tradition of rebellion (just as, with no experience of the sea or a voyage, that little caique was suspended on wires from the ceiling in front of the Virgin of Kykko). An adult logic that made us recognize that the *Saint George* had taken more than one trip was more crucial than the fate of the five or six men on trial.

This militant maturity (which perhaps, I confess, was due to our own childish recklessness, if you simply dismiss it as such, then you don't understand how much the movement owed to our recklessness and impetuosity) grew during the struggle to a surprising degree, so that in the end we were completely (there was no hyperbole in that "completely") cut off from parents, siblings, friends, in short, from the entire world of normal childhood. Plato must have been a child like us in a world like ours, in which the explosion was not a continuation of previous explosions, but an explosion which sprang from a perfect calm as when one splits the center of an atom, when he wrote that the country must be placed above everything else, even one's father and mother.

When the sentences for the crew of the *Saint George* were finally announced in court, the judge "took into account" Koutalianos's commendation. (What was this "took into account"?) (Was this the kind of commendation maids took with them when they sought new employment?) They took under consideration his "conduct" during the war. (Was "conduct" a euphemism for risking one's life?) And in court they sentenced the captain, as opposed to the others, to only four years of prison. (You mean the former comrades-in-arms did open their hearts to the captain? "Read the paper again.")

"Are such men to pass judgment upon Koutalianos?" we asked. But the sound of our voices surprised us, it was not in the tone we expected, it had no outrage or indignation. It did not seem recognizable as our old voice at all. And we were suddenly ashamed of the innocence of our old voice, and of the tears we once had shed over the commendation with our father, with Cyprus, and with Greece (forget it, don't even discuss it).

The truth was that now we were no longer concerned, as we had been before, with the fate of the accused; the trial no longer occupied our thoughts. We hardly had time to discuss the verdicts; "Are such men to pass judgment on Koutalianos?" was about all the reaction we could manage. Nor did we have time to discuss the sentences (was it even a good thing that we asked "are such men to judge Koutalianos?") because only a few days before the decisions were handed down in the courtroom, the armed revolution had started.

13

I MUST TELL YOU that a lot of the grown-ups expressed the opinion that the revolution should not have begun until the verdicts were announced. We children (and I have analyzed how we felt, how quickly we adjusted to the course of events) found nothing to criticize.

"How can a revolution wait for five men?"

What? Were we willing to sacrifice our Koutalianos? Yes, we sacrificed him without any hesitation, along with the heroic stories we had constructed about him, and the tales of our grandmothers that he aroused in our memories, and the faded photographs in the old barbershops. Along with him, we now sacrificed everything and everyone (underline that "now" in bold relief).

I would always remember that night with a strange feeling of swelling in my chest (I used this image before) like the swell of waves on the beach at Kyrenia in the summer. For hours I would sit on the jetty and watch the waves stretch to their full height, rising up for the final, desperate effort, something like the last spark flaring up, before crashing and breaking on the rocks. It did not seem to matter that the sparks would return, in other forms; the significant fact was they had to rise up and face their special end like waves, like fire, to write their own story very real on the rock.

It was April 1st, April Fool's Day, but it was no playful April Fool's Day lie or prank that we heard. One, two, three, many frightening explosions, followed by several more, shook the windows of the houses and the blue, clear, peaceful night. People poured into the street. (Did you say a peaceful night? Who bothered to look?)

"What was that?"

"They must have been bombs" (Bombs? Bombs! Again the Greek Revolution thundered suddenly and we recalled the eyebrows of Kolokotronis, once again he enveloped us in his wild, bushy eyebrows, as he shot a rifle at the stars).

"No, it was dynamite," said someone who had worked for many years as a foreman at the Skouriotissa Mine, and knew the sound.

Bombs! Dynamite! So there were men to take up arms after all! Let those who had doubts take a good look now! Something flapped its wings inside of me, what I'm not sure, and I felt something like a tear (a tear?) burning my eyes, filling my eyes and staying there without overflowing or dissipating. Such tears don't pour out, they aren't wasted in crying. It is as if they remained on the edge for many hours to renew themselves all on their own, and are still able to rise up now if I let myself go. (But let's move on, we'll come back to it. Let's not betray the story with gaps in time or lapses in logic. So that's how it was? Yes, just so. And fifteen years old? Yes, fifteen.)

You said for those who had doubts to take a good look now? Who were they? "They" no longer existed. Among the diverse crowd suddenly filling the streets, half asleep, half dressed, wandering aimlessly. I knew right away that I would not find a single man to ask, on behalf of us children, "Did you see who did it?" The crowd filling the streets was not composed of people that I knew, they were strangers. ("Beware of who you talk to." "What were you saying about arms?" "What arms?") Perhaps, as I said earlier, some, even many, had received the news of the *Saint George* in January with doubts/misgivings, but they accepted the evening bombs that April 1st like the fireworks of Easter. And who has misgivings about Easter? You could say that the crowd came into the street as it went into the churchyard at Easter, with the glittering of candles and eyes, with souls ready to hear the joyful news. So these people, who had for hundreds of years hardly seen a gun or blood on their soil, welcomed the first bombs.

The sky, carrying the sound of detonations, mingled with us on the street, shoved its way in between people as a child does, to overhear the conversations (loud, abrupt phrases in which the words were not formed into sentences) filling the empty air.

"God help them," said the women, and most of them wept. (No, it was not the bombs that raised the standard of Revolution that night, but the people in the street who held it aloft.)

"God protect them."

("Them"? Who were "they"? We did not know, no one knew. It might be their children, their brothers, their own husbands for whom they prayed.)

15

NO ONE IN OUR NEIGHBORHOOD could say where the bombs had gone off or where the dynamite had been placed. But in the dreamlike calm of that April night the concept of space had so shrunk that all of Nicosia seemed without sections or neighborhoods (out of necessity I confine myself to speak only of Nicosia). You had the sense that the explosions had occurred just outside your front door, that they banged on your door and asked you to come outside so that they could tell you something.

Only the next day did we learn anything.

"In such different places." "So far apart." "It's curious."

And the next day we read the first mimeographed leaflets that were found scattered on the streets. It announced that "with God's help, with faith in the justice of the cause . . ." Below was the signature that would become so well-known and dear to us. "EOKA, the leader Dighenis." (Did we find it scattered in the streets? No, that first leaflet leapt suddenly during the night straight into our rooms, just as the dynamite had, and we jumped out of bed at the noise. "Are you ready?" "We are ready!")

At first we scanned the leaflet quickly, it all seemed one word, one syllable. We read it later slowly and carefully, in seclusion we bent over it and confronted it eye to eye, so to speak. We read it again a third, fourth, fifth time. Afterwards, we looked at it "from both sides" without reading it (you must have seen similar interruptions during children's games, when a lapse occurs, a subconscious attempt to analyze, to quantify, to recapture something like one's New Year's Day happiness?). We communicated with the leaflet by touch, at firsthand, as if by osmosis. (And the same way looking with the eyes? Yes, an osmosis of the eyes as well.) And little by little, it began to swell, to breathe, to lodge itself inside of us. We did not speak any longer; everything suddenly turned inwards. Did this mean that somewhere within us we still had not believed even after the explosions, and only now could we assimilate everything, only now could we take in the full significance of the model hanging by wires in front of the Virgin in the monastery of Kykko? Perhaps (it came to us slowly, I admit) it had nothing to do with a storm at sea. I don't know, but it is my purpose to record everything as I remember it.

16

We took a long time to fully comprehend the details of the leaflet. EOKA. E–O–K–A. We tried to find from what words (golden lucky words) the beautiful name had been formed. EOKA. Where had it hidden for so many centuries, waiting for a belated little island to find it? Why had it never crept into the stories of grandmothers; why had it not been part of the whispers of the night?

Then when the first shock had subsided (not "shock" really, something else) our great questions began. Not quite "began," rather we took things up in a kind of order, and these next questions succeeded the earlier ones. Who made up this EOKA? Who was this Dighenis?

Dighenis? First Koutalianos, and now Dighenis? No, it could not be a real name this time, two such coincidences were not possible. But really, who could have dared to take the name of the greatest hero of our childhood fantasies, the name of the one who had wrestled for forty days on the iron threshing-floor with Death himself and won the match? ("Where Dighenis grasps, the blood begins to spurt," the old song went.) And he was not just a fairy tale hero, but had a very real presence on our island. Had we not ourselves seen the rock he threw into the sea near the harbor of Paphos, when Rigena broke her promise and refused to marry him? Had he not thrown his heart into the sea with the rock to meet the waves beyond the limits of land, to wrestle naked with the waves? We knew the places where he walked, under the places where he had frowned. Grandmother, in tales passed down from mouth to mouth, tales without a single blot of ink on them, had brought his song, his voice and his lance to life. He was truly ours, completely ours.

How could we have known, how could we have even suspected, no matter how childish or intoxicated we might have been, that such a legendary name would not be grand enough for our new hero? How could we have known, or even guessed, that for four years this EOKA and the leader Dighenis would capture not only our young minds, but the imagination of millions of people throughout the world? When we read that first leaflet, how could we have known, who would ever have believed, that even our new Dighenis would also wrestle with Death and win? ("Where Dighenis grasps, . . .")

How could we have known it? I am lying, for we knew it. Perhaps the adults did not (even though I said just above

17

that the first night of the bombs had elided the distinction between grown-ups and children). We gave ourselves, heart and
soul, to that leaflet from the first moment. We believed in it
right away. We believed in Dighenis. We believed in threshing floors. We swore an oath to that leaflet, we made it a part
of us, we bound it in our handkerchiefs and pinned it to our
hearts. Later we crumpled it in our fists when the pain of torture made us dig our nails into our palms. We held hands with
it and together we rushed to scratch with fingernails against the
machine guns. From the beginning to the end. Nothing in
between so influenced us, nothing in between was able to
shake our faith.

"With God's help."

FROM THAT NIGHT, we regularly heard the bombs and dynamite. As soon as darkness fell, the noise began. We all waited impatiently to hear the explosions, and we grew anxious if they were delayed. We children were not simply nervous, we were in agony. A curious kind of agony, even greater than when we were quite small and would wait for the overdue knock of our mother upon the door after she had promised us that she would return early and we were alone in the house as the sun began to set. Occasionally the bombs were so late we would no longer be able to fight off the sweet insistence of sleep (as long as we could resist, just another moment more), no matter how hard we resisted. We nodded off only to awaken in an instant at the sound of the blasts, into that same half-sleeping state we used to have in our early childhood on Christmas Eve when we waited to hear the bells ring, so that we could wake our mother before she came for us. (No, we did not wake our mother. Later she told us that many times she had in fact woken before us, but pretended to sleep to give us the joy of coming to her. And when we did not appear, and it seemed as if we would sleep through the bells, she tried with noises, slight nudges, and a thousand tricks to rouse us so that we, in turn, could wake her up.)

When finally the long anticipated explosions shook the air we would scream with relief and jump up in our beds; it wasn't a gentle rousing, you can add to our relief that our agony did not let us rest quietly. We held onto it tightly so sleep could not take us; we held on to it, unlike other anxieties that put their grip on us. We held it as we used to grasp a New Year's toy in bed with us and if anyone so much as touched it we awakened immediately. (How did we manage to guard it so vigilantly?)

"Mother! Father! Did you hear that?"

Of course they heard it.

"Yes." (A long drawn out "yes" like a trickle of water on a field, whispered, without vowels, after midnight, deep from within, a "yes" that says everything, a "yes" that echoes like the sudden opening of a tightly closed spigot.) After the yes, a complete silence in the house. Concentrated listening. The rooms were tip-toeing.

"Another one!"

"Yes" (the same "yes").

19

I said the explosions shook the air, but it was not exactly like that. It was something different. You had the sense that these ephemeral April nights, the satin sky, and the blossoming almond trees; I don't know how to say it, but you had the sense that they opened up their arms to the bombs to provide them a place in which to hide, and then closed around the explosions so that no harm might come to Spring.

MEANWHILE, we had our first casualty. This first one, I admit, made us question our commitment.

"The poor fellow. How did it happen?"

Despite our enthusiasm for the cause, we were unprepared for casualties. Deaths are difficult to accept when you have not had them for centuries.

You stop suddenly to take another look, to reassess the situation. Perhaps tomorrow it might be your brother, or even you yourself? Yes, perhaps. The war stories you had read as a boy seized this moment to parade before you; dismembered bodies with severed legs, eyes glazed over, bullet holes in the foreheads of handsome blonde youths. (Such things as that here on the island? Yes, those very things. What do you think of all this now? The eyebrows of Kolokotronis darkened a bit, the sword of Dhiakos and the Inn of Gravia dimmed.)

Nevertheless we passed through that stage quickly (surprisingly quickly). It had to happen quickly, actually, for we had no time to wait for the usual progression, the protracted stages, the complicated process of normal changes. Just put all that aside. Even the stories and pictures of war no longer found fertile ground in our minds, they managed to disturb us just once or twice. We soon became less queasy about spilled blood, that holy fluid that matters when nothing else matters, and controls (who knows for how long?) the harsh fate of humans. Who knew how long it would be before he might pay the ultimate penalty at great moments, to close with red finality the open questions, to cut away the small pretexts? ("Very well, I'll pay.") I can't say that such phrases as "the poor fellow" or "how did it happen" vanished from conversation, but they definitely took second place. They remained inside of us; they withdrew into a subconscious space, into the region of our private logic and private worlds (again to pierce the ceiling with the wide-open eyes and to hear the kri-kri of the cricket in the corner—that's a completely different matter), and they left the struggle undisturbed.

THE ENGLISH were taken by surprise—how could they not have been surprised when we ourselves, those of us who were not initiated into EOKA's secret organization, were completely caught off guard at first. Even after the *Saint George* affair, we were continually amazed by events on each succeeding day. As if it were a slow, deliberate crescendo. So the revolution spread through the cities and villages, the mountains and plains. It encompassed the old and the young—men, women, and children, knocking on doors and climbing on roofs, announcing its progress. The English were at loss as to how to deal with it and, in their confusion, they increased the already large number of troops on the island and kept sending more and more.

Besides, everything was so incomprehensible to the English that at first they simply could not admit that the revolutionaries might be Cypriots. They talked of "agitators" who had come from Greece. This was understandable, actually, since enough of us Cypriots held the same opinion, a conviction that grew as the actions of the "agitators" became more daring. I do not quite understand the reasoning; I do not see why daring has to be traditional.

We children (again I speak particularly about children without realizing it, however much I might mention the adults) were not amused at all at the idea that the rebels had come from Greece, however much we came to admire the Greeks from our readings in school. We wanted those who took up arms to be Cypriots. You remember that I spoke of how that word echoed upon, exploded upon, our servitude? How could we envision those arms in the hands of others? After so many centuries they were coming to us, were coming for us, in our own name. No one else should touch them. We wanted all of the fighters to be Cypriots, even Dighenis. No, especially Dighenis. Perhaps we were overwhelmed by provincial pride; children are quite susceptible to provincial pride, because whether they were Greeks or Cypriots we wanted to claim them "all," and, besides, there was need for experience we did not have. Perhaps we thought that Greece already had her fair share of glorious events, and that we should take this one for ourselves. (You have to understand, this was a special case. We didn't want to be left out of the dance of Roumeli, of the Morea, and of Crete. We would find a way to obtain experience; we would use other means in place of experience.)

22

We wanted them to be Cypriots so badly that we wouldn't here any arguments to the contrary. (Haven't you observed these strange reactions?)

"They are all (All!) Cypriots."

Nevertheless, deep inside of us we were uneasy; we must have doubted it, because the first thing we always asked when someone had been killed was:

"Was he a Cypriot?"

"Yes."

We had no further questions. We were relieved by the "yes." We managed to feel joy in the sorrowful news (I told you, don't be afraid of words). We set that "yes" beside the "yes" of our parents on the first nights when the bombs woke us from sleep. (Concerning the "yes," I don't remember, did I say that it had something childlike, very childlike, even though, as we asked ourselves earlier, where does childhood begin?)

A few months later, no one doubted that the resistance fighters were all Cypriots. Even the English admitted it when they triumphantly announced that they had discovered the true identity of Dighenis—he was a Cypriot. Did the English ever realize what joy their "triumph" provided to us?

"Didn't we tell you all along? Even Dighenis himself."

BESIDES THE ADDITIONAL TROOPS the English kept bringing to the island, they created a force of local Turks called "the auxiliary police," whom they incited with fears. (They knew exactly how to manufacture such feelings—hadn't they done so in similar circumstances in India and other places in their empire?) They gathered whatever Turks would volunteer —literate or illiterate, honest men or rogues and ex-convicts.

We observed the auxiliary police wrapped up in barbed wire (they were wrapped up in it just after the first bombs—I should have mentioned this at the very beginning, but the memories started to come back all at once and confused me). And when we saw all that barbed wire, all those Turks, all that vigilance, all that intensity, it reminded us how, when we were little, we snuggled down into our beds to get away from the cold, or covered our heads with blankets from fear of the dark. And we swelled up with pride.

"They are afraid of us!" (You know what that "they are afraid" means to children, how it affects them? You know, you must know, how they are ready to pay dearly for it.)

"They are terrorized!" (Let that word pass this once, don't use it again. *They* will call, they have already called, your struggle for liberty "terrorism.")

The truth is, and it was apparent at the time, that the English immediately took the rebellion seriously. Perhaps the Intelligence Service had detected the depth of the resistance, or perhaps the global atmosphere and the possible repercussions in other regions made the English pay attention to the revolt on the island (it is fitting to note that the biggest mistakes occur when one decides to pay attention). They no longer expressed the contempt that they knew how to express so very well. They were no longer concerned about their sense of superiority as they had always been. (What about those Cypriots now?)

Nevertheless, in spite of all of those English troops, all of the auxiliary policemen, all of the emergency measures, and all of the censorship, every day the newspapers were filled with activities of EOKA. The papers came each morning as if still warm from the presses, as if breathless from haste, to bring us the news from across the island. How we seized and devoured them. And, even with censorship, they managed with a hint or wink, by a certain emphasis or insinuation, to tell us what we were dying to know ("Tell us. . . . Well? Are you going to?").

Then there was the radio. We laid siege to it morning, noon, and night, listening to the latest bulletins from Cyprus Radio and all the foreign stations we could receive—Athens, London, Cairo, Moscow. In our house, my father and Nikos, who both knew English, would get up by six to hear the first broadcast from London. If there was anything important they would run and wake us. And if they did not come for us, then we rushed down to them as soon as we got up.

"What is London saying?"

I remember that before the struggle my father's first concern every morning had been whether or not it would rain. Rain had been the great preoccupation of the whole island for centuries.

"Will we have rain this year?"

That was the standard question asked millions of times by millions of people. (I know that such phrases cannot be called traditional, but can they not become something else, what? No, it wasn't possible to add a word to the question, or to change the order of words used.)

"Will we have rain this year?" (How can you add a word or change a word? Wouldn't it confuse the mountains, who asked the question in their own way, or the plains, who brooded over the question in the heat of midday, or the gray owls who hooted it at night from the ruins of old mills?)

And when in December the clear sky showed no signs of clouds, the prayers and processions began in the churches and chapels to end the drought, to stop the curse of blue. The people filled the churches; they made all-night vigils so that the little iron-roofed chapel in the ravine at Molivoskepasti almost seemed haunted at night, the priest appeared to be a ghost, the candles from another world. People climbed to the inaccessible peak of Tripylos and beseeched the aid of the Prophet Elijah. (We had not prayed to him for some time, but here on the heights we could always find him, may his name be praised.)

Eyes nailed to the sky, hanging on the hope of some cloud that appeared on the horizon, we watched as one swelled quickly, then drew near and passed over our heads without stopping (like a formation of cranes), without even stopping to look down (the cranes never look down), and then disappeared like an empty dream. Sometimes a cloud halted for a second and spread, spread and covered the sky and gave us wings. It

25

might even stay for a day or two playing with our emotions, and we watched it in agony until, on the second or third night, it picked itself up and fled quietly, just like the cruel prince. And we would awake in the morning to find it gone and ourselves plunged again into the blue left behind (as in the story Myrsinia awoke alone in the morning and ran frantically after the prince to collapse on the white dust of the road).

"Cursed place."

"Don't blaspheme," the women admonished.

The frightened people began to remember the great droughts of the past, poring through history to learn about the seventeen years when it had not rained even a drop and all the inhabitants were forced to abandon the island.

The newspapers attempted to console us by referring to the cyclical weather patterns in the medieval Chronicle of Machairas, and published the reassuring opinions of the elders.

"It will rain. The harvest is just a bit late this year."

Father looked to the distant violet mass of the Troodos range, and to the rocks of the Pentadactylos mountains, towards the East.

"Nothing. Nothing."

The drought became a serious matter for him. He was not simply upset, he was obsessed, he became a bit psychotic. And little by little, with daily contact, he infected us with his psychosis. As soon as we awoke and we saw the fiery sun through our shutters, we grew melancholy.

"Summer again today."

In order to be sure (you never know), we ran to the window half-naked and slowly opened the curtains (it was always the first thing we did in the morning) trying to avoid direct eye contact with the blue curse (just as when you hesitate to look beneath a rock you have just picked up for fear of what evil might be under it).

But as soon as the struggle began, we forgot all about the rain, we pushed it to the side for some other time. Our first concern in the mornings was not to look at the sky, but to nail our ears to the radio.

"What is he saying?" We interrupted the English news bulletin impatiently if a familiar word like Cyprus, Famagusta, or Limassol was heard.

"Sssh. Wait till the end." (Wait? How could we wait? "A Battle?" "Sssh.")

26

What we heard from the London and Nicosia stations, the exact words, was hardly taken at face value. It wasn't difficult for us to learn rapidly how British propaganda worked, both what it was trying to suggest and what it was trying to conceal. So little had its methods changed (and not simply the methods, the phrasing never changed either), so monotonously childish were the efforts, that we used to shout at the radio: "Tell us something we don't know!" I remember reading a pamphlet that compared British propaganda in Ireland in 1921 to that employed in Cyprus thirty-four years later. It examined the texts of official announcements and investigated the application of emergency actions and measures, and concluded that hardly any differences existed between the two cases, hardly any development could be found from 1921 to 1955. It demonstrated convincingly that no difference existed between the two, no progress had been made, not a single lesson had been learned.

Although we knew what to expect, every now and then we became exasperated (even patience has limits).

"I want to make a fist and smash the radio into a thousand pieces!"

But how could we smash the radio into a thousand pieces when it also brought us the voice of Athens? Athens? Never had the name had such special connotations. When we heard the seductive opening of the Voice of Athens broadcast ("Aderfoi Kyprioi"—how to translate that—"brother Cypriots" seems too bland. No, "our Cypriots," much better) we held our breath. (No, we did not really hold our breath. For this instance, we needed to find a new phrase to describe our reaction, something never used before.)

"Sssh."

The radio seemed to rise off the table, to hover somewhere above us. Sometimes we felt as if we clutched the radio to our breasts so that it could speak to us as closely as possible, that its warmth caressed us and we could hear its heart beat (heart listening to heart). "Our Cypriots." Yes, tell us again that we have become worthy of Greece! Tell us!

I heard an anecdote about the Athens broadcast which a neighbor who worked for a cooperative related to us.

He had gone with a delegation to escort a representative from the Dutch cooperative movement to visit a rural cooperative market (a fine time he chose to visit Cyprus). They

27

had just arrived at the market, barely taken their seats in fact, the Dutchman was just pulling out his notebook to ask the first question to get down to business (was this a time for such things?), when the secretary who had been looking anxiously at his watch jumped up.

"Excuse me, it is time for Athens." (Time for Athens? Who can make us a song with this verse as the refrain?) "Come back in the afternoon. I cannot talk now. *Holy hour*," he added in broken English to the puzzled foreigner ("*Holy hour*?" Where did he learn this phrase?).

He left the room. (How could he talk about cooperatives when the radio was about to lift off the table?)

"*What's all this about*?" the visitor asked his escort in English.

"*Athens*," our neighbor replied with bemusement.

"*Athens*?"

"*Yes, he told you. Holy hour.*"

It is worth repeating another story about Athens radio, since the British so insistently claimed that it spread lies. One day the Athenian "News from Cyprus" reported an incident from the village of Lapithos (how many memories come to me at the mention of that name, the village of my father's youth, a place half-sea and half- mountain, with one foot in the sand of the beach of Airkotissa, and the other in the water mills of Kephalovriso where the Nereids still dwell). Well, in Lapithos, the broadcast said, five villagers had been buried alive in the sand during an interrogation. This was, it turned out, not true. The English Information Office proved that by questioning the inhabitants. "Are you certain this never happened?" "No, it did not happen." The next day, Cyprus Radio provocatively announced the following challenge.

"Tomorrow at nine in the morning the Commissioner of Nicosia will be in Kyrenia to take depositions about the burial of five villagers of Lapithos, as asserted by Athens radio. Anyone who has any information at all is invited to be present to make a statement."

The Commissioner left for Kyrenia in the morning confident that no one would appear, and was completely startled to find ten villagers waiting for him.

"What do they want?"

"To make a statement."

They had come to give depositions that they had all been buried alive during interrogations. They spoke with an assured air and quiet conviction.

It did not happen, of course, in Lapithos, but they thought that . . .

"Wait."

They waited for a long time before they were finally given an answer.

"No, you cannot make a deposition today." (How well we came to understand their "today," or their "for the time being," just as, over time, we came to know their "I can see no way" and their "It will serve no purpose," and a thousand other such things. Expressions from a foggy northern country, political spin with no relation to our lives.) They could not give a deposition "today."

I don't know if Athens had sincerely made a mistake about the name of the village, or had done so intentionally to mislead the British. Whatever the case, the story offers further proof about the amazing simple-mindedness of the British attempts at propaganda.

IN ADDITION to the newspapers and the radio, we received news from the contraband "leaflets." These came from another world—no not quite another world, but from within us, out of our sleeplessness, our wide-open eyes that pierced the ceiling. We did not write or distribute them, but somehow we felt they were a part of us and we had a hand in their creation. And we spoke about them all day long; wherever you went, people talked about the leaflets. The barber shop always had one hidden away for clients, the coffee shop had one for customers, everyone had one at home to share with neighbors. They were taken out of shoes, out of shirts, out of shirtsleeves; just sweaty, soiled, wrinkled, almost illegible bits of paper, but your soul always made the sign of the cross before unfolding one of them. It made the sign of the cross because it knew what these insignificant scraps of paper represented, who sent them, what eons lay behind them, what oceans they had crossed, what messages they carried.

Now conversations no longer began with a mention of business or the weather (all these things, like father's rain, had been swept away) but always with the struggle, and the leaflets provided a ready opening.

"Do you have the new leaflet?"

It was as though these leaflets were falling from the sky. They fluttered down upon you from nowhere, sent by no visible hand, into streets, churches, movie theaters, schools, hotels, coffee shops, restaurants, stores, buses. You would suddenly see them glued on walls, doors, windows, even cars. They were everywhere. You woke in the morning and Nicosia was full of leaflets (I am speaking of Nicosia, but it was the same in Limassol, in Famagusta, in Larnaca, in Kyrenia, in Paphos, in Marathasa, in Soli, in Mesaoria, in Karpasia). Nothing could stop them, certainly not the blackouts nor the curfews (we will talk about the curfews). When it was time for them to appear, they would appear, even if the world came to an end.

If the police were not close by, the public picked up the leaflets in an instant (an instant, no more). It was quite a sight to see people silently rush toward them like ants. How silently, without a word, they would hide them with a well-rehearsed, rapid movement. Each one developed his or her own personal way of folding and concealing a leaflet. Then

they immediately scattered feigning indifference and igno-
rance.

Frequently, however, a security patrol would be on
hand to gather them up first. This turned out to be a slow, la-
borious process that could take hours. The soldiers had to
count the leaflets one by one to have a total for their report,
and the total had to match the number of leaflets handed over
to their commander. They collected the leaflets amidst a continual, shrill whistling that enraged the soldiers. They could
never tell exactly where the whistling came from—roofs,
stores, balconies, the air, and the sky were all whistling, even
the asphalt.

"*Shut Up!*" the soldiers yelled in English. The whistling would get louder.

"*Shut Up!*" (To whom did you yell it? The sky?)

You could see the veins on the necks of the soldiers become red and enlarged, as if they would burst.

Later, collecting the leaflets became a dangerous task.
While the soldiers were occupied picking up the papers, a hand
grenade might drop among them, or perhaps a burst of machine gun fire. So, naturally, they changed tactics and had
passing civilians collect the leaflets for them. And when these
passers-by were children, like we were, they inevitably managed to conceal two or three.

"Our commission," they said and laughed.

And those who succeeded in taking a leaflet, I remember how they ran to hide and read it. They ran? No, they did
not run. They were coiled around that precious piece of paper
so that they could feel it in their shoes as they walked ever so
lightly, or squeezed it in their bosoms and were afraid to
breathe deeply for fear it might fall out.

To read it, yes, but then breathlessly to pass it on, to
hand it over like a lighted torch.

"I've brought a leaflet!" (I have used a lot of exclama-
tion marks in this story. But take a second, think about that
phrase and ponder it.)

They resembled toddlers who find something in the
street and, grasping it tightly in their hands, run to their
mother to open their handkerchief and let the little piece of
joy, which they had held so closely, pour out before her (Be
patient, we're here). But inside they felt like the Marathon

runner who brought word of the great victory (Don't hesitate to make the comparison).

"I've brought a leaflet!" (Ponder it, we said.)

Along with the chore of gathering up the leaflets, I should also mention that the soldiers would force the passers-by to erase with black paint the slogans written on the pavement of the street. Men on their way to work had to get down on their hands and knees, to remove their jackets and ties, to perform this task. These slogans were also on walls, on traffic signs, on telephone poles, on mailboxes. And then there were the banners that spread in half a second on all the downtown streets or were put on trees and the peaks of mountains wherever you went.

ALTHOUGH WITHOUT PARENTHESES (are you tired of them?) we are still at the beginning of the struggle (I don't know if I have confused you), I have to say a few more things about the distribution of the leaflets. The leaflets continued to appear without interruption in time or supply throughout the strictest emergency measures. In the worst phase, the soldiers no longer simply arrested Cypriots caught dispersing the leaflets for interrogation and imprisonment. The security forces now shot and killed violators on the spot (*"Shoot to kill"* became the order of the day. They announced this *"Shoot to Kill"* policy and then enforced it without mercy. "Not at the feet! Kill them!" And "they" were two small schoolgirls with the ordinary, turned up school caps (Don't let anyone change the design of those caps. Why is there no statue of the little girl with the twisted, turned up cap?). Or "they" were two little boys in their school uniforms on their way home. (Why is there no statue of the little boy in his uniform in Tapia?) Yes, yes, not at the feet (what good is it to stop the feet?). Shoot at the heart, because the heart, the little, tiny but huge, wonderful heart of a small, but amazing child, had dared, had defied logic, had shown the way).

"Shoot to kill." Whom did they want to frighten? We heard a story about a twelve-year-old girl who was caught distributing pamphlets. When they told her father, a superior court employee, to come to the police station, his eyes popped right out of his head.

"But my daughter is afraid of her own shadow!"

"We caught her!," retorted the English officer.

And it was true that this fearful little girl (who was afraid of her own shadow) had taken it upon herself to distribute leaflets. (What hope had the English after that?)

Another twelve-year-old girl from Strovolos, on the night of the Easter service, secretly left the church to distribute leaflets to a monastery three miles away, three miles on foot across dark fields and olive groves, planted with patrols of English soldiers and Turkish auxiliaries.

I must tell you how, a few years into the revolt, the English began to produce and spread their own "illegal" leaflets (it was one of their more laughable efforts of propaganda). They contrived a meaningless signature, then circulated them secretly, mysteriously and "unlawfully," as if they were the real thing. Only these were left fluttering about, they were not gathered up by the security forces (the people called them the forces of insecurity), nor were the civilians forced to pick them up. The soldiers actually stood by to "guard" them. And you should have seen the anticipation on the faces of these guards as they waited impatiently for someone to pick one up.

It was comical. And it became even more ludicrous when, as the pedestrians did not touch them (they observed them, if they observed them at all, out of the corner of an eye—they weren't worth a whole eye), a young soldier would push a leaflet toward them with his foot and yell:

"*There!*"

Now we would toy with such soldiers in two ways. Either we took one, and without looking at it, immediately crumpled it up and threw it back in the street, or we answered his "*there*" with a firm "*no.*"

"*Bloody fool!*," they screamed at us.

It was all so funny. But who knew the person behind the voice that shouted "*there*"? Who knew anything about the soldier with whom we toyed (either John with the blue eyes, or Charles with the pointed red nose), who was called up for their military service and suddenly found himself in this terrible situation where he did not know who the enemy was, could not tell where a bullet came from, in which tree (a blossoming tree with all its foliage—"*Look at that beautiful tree!*") a bomb was about to explode, under what bridge a car of gunmen waited, nor which smile was a real smile, which woman a real woman, or which child a real child (a child like Dennis, your sister's boy, to kiss on the head—see what golden hair he has!). Who knew who had made the soldiers believe that if those leaflets circulated, if the people read them, the situation would change? Who knew what had been said to them about a few "terrorists" (who invented this word?) and the common people were "forced to collaborate out of fear?" Who knew how the soldiers were lied to, how their ability to see clearly was impaired, how their perceptions were distorted?

We toyed with them without knowing whom we made fun of, without thinking that they had mothers, wives, children, or fiancées waiting for them to return. (The photograph is in his pocket, or nailed to the wall near his bed. Just yesterday he had stared at it for hours. "Why hasn't a letter come yet?" And he daydreamed.)

34

(We toyed with them? Was it we who toyed with them, we who fooled them? No, it was their own government, their own people, who toyed with them.)

What was even more comical was when some curious person (perhaps he wasn't curious but took it in order to turn it over to the Organization) did not step over the leaflet but took it to read (without precautions, what was there to fear?) and a different patrol (in which no one knew Greek) dragged him to the police station where, to the amazement of the soldiers, the commander was furious and yelled at them.

"You stupid! You spoil everything! Let him go!"

After that (I am beginning to think you won't believe me) the one or two who took the English counterfeit leaflets would hide them just as carefully as they would conceal the real ones (only they would not step gently when the paper was in their shoe, they would stomp on it). And I will stretch my credibility even further when I say that many times the counterfeit leaflets were printed on paper bearing the Crown's stamp (What was going on? For whom were these people working? England?).

But it was downright pathetic when the English soldiers went from house to house, distributing not the counterfeit leaflets, but the genuine ones from Dighenis. They came to the door of our house and begged us to take a leaflet to read with a look in their eyes which was hard to reject. ("Just read and see.") And because of the sincerity of that look (the look on the faces of John and Charles) we did not refuse (and why should we, after all they were not the counterfeit leaflets at all). So I repeat. What was going on? Did the people who sent the soldiers on such a task work for England?

The English were not content to make up counterfeit leaflets, they also painted the town with counterfeit slogans. I will talk more about this later. But they were not able to fool anyone. Our leaflets were not leaflets, they were hearts, hearts for which you cannot make copies—real or counterfeit. EOKA did not write with ink, it wrote with our blood. And did EOKA even write the words? No, they had already been written four thousand years earlier. How could they fool us? How could our instincts be fooled?

THERE WAS ALSO A WAR against the English language—against English road signs, English street names, stores with English names. The war was to completely eliminate their language from our daily life, to eliminate anything that reminded us of the English, to uncover our language just as we had uncovered the mosaic in Saint Mary Aggeloktisi at Kition under the whitewash painted over it by the Turks.

For us, everything on the island suddenly breathed Greek, sang Greek. Only as if in some distant nightmare did we half remember that the sign which now read "Chrysopsaro" had once been *The Golden Fish*," or the "Nereidon Kastron" *"The Fairy Castle."*

The English retaliated (their pride would not allow them not to retaliate). They responded with smears of black paint, and by targeting shops that had only Greek signs in blue. They responded with English obscenities on walls and lewd drawings on painted Greek flags.

EVERY EVENING AT HOME we discussed the situation (we all participated, we were all well versed in the subject). Each one related what he or she had seen or heard that day. My mother no longer sat with her knitting, my father no longer had time for his stamps, we children no longer wrote our lessons. Homework? We took our books in our hands, if in fact we touched a book, but they felt like something foreign, from another place and time, like a useless memory of a bygone era. ("How many years ago was it that I looked at that?") The letters in the books were hazy, the tales of ancient bravery meaningless. It was the worst possible time to read heroic tales of other people, other places. The stories seemed irrelevant, incapable of any relation to our present. Or our enthusiasm for our struggle was so blind that it would admit of no comparisons or analogies (What has the French Revolution to do with us now!). And later when the heroic resistance, the famous "no," came from Afxentiou, and from Matsis, and from the four fighters in Liopetri, we would not allow any kind of comparisons at all, even with such beloved names as Thermopylae or Maniaki.

"There were three hundred at Thermopylae, but Afxentiou was all alone. Consider the psychological aspect. Afxentiou had no one else to lean upon, no company but his own shadow, nothing to listen to but his own voice."

But why "later"? No one knows at what moment Afxentiou came, or Matsis, or the heroes of Liopetri. Such events do not come about in seconds, but in centuries. They are not programmed or subject to time. They were present on the first of April, from the first leaflet, from the beginning of time.

Books? What books? We had other things on our minds now, our strikes at school, our demonstrations, our collisions with the security forces. In these confrontations the English sharpened and shaped us. The English never realized that they were, in fact, training us for incorporation into the armed resistance.

The collisions began (we have drifted away from the discussions at home—let's leave aside those static evenings in the house for a moment) when, all of a sudden, we would pour out of school on to the streets with a large, provocative flag at the front, wildly flapping like a crazy, excited, impetuous child, exactly like the children following it, if you like. We never even acknowledged the teachers who tried to restrain us. Their voices never reached our ears, they stayed at the level of our feet, and our feet, at that moment, trampled upon anything in their way. (We didn't even recognize the teachers? Who were they?) Do you remember the story of the Pied Piper from the English reader in school? (Had they not translated for us the Pied Piper?) You remember how with his pipe he could make the children rush uncontrollably after him? It was that way with us.

We knew that somewhere the English were waiting for us. They were waiting with riot-gear, as they called it—helmets, shields, clubs, tear gas. The helmets and shields reminded us, in our childish excitement, of the Persians (is this a satire on history?), of Darius and Xerxes, and we rushed at them for both the recent and ancient wrongs ("March, children of Greece," sang the ancient poet) and assaulted them with rocks, pots, bottles, fists, kicks, fingernails, and, above all, with a great hatred, a strange, enormous hatred mixed with a haughty contempt. (The contempt did not always follow or replace the hatred even at its peak, rather the two often merged into a fearful alloy.)

Almost always the schoolgirls joined us. They were no longer schoolgirls, no longer girls at all. Even when the English began to open fire on the crowd, they rushed forward recklessly with their small voices increasing in decibels and pitch. When they joined the fray, we boys fought even harder, inspired by these unyielding, committed cries. When the battle for their flag raged, the battle for our own paled in comparison. They kicked, scratched with their nails, and bit with a fury the hands that tried to pull away their staff. (It seems more difficult to take a flag away from a woman than from a man. Perhaps she has fewer means of making a protest, fewer opportunities to join the battle.) The English hit at them unmercifully with clubs and the butts of their weapons, and they tore out their hair by the roots.

When the tear gas came, we retreated to take up positions to throw stones. The English feared the stones, especially at the start, before they had thought of using helmets or shields. In their bewilderment at the assault, they often abandoned the tear gas ("Leave it alone") and threw the stones back at us. We would remember later and laugh about how they would awkwardly bend down, jerk up again, contort their bodies, and, of course, miss their mark. Aim? They could never manage to hit anything, even after, according to the newspapers, they had taken special training in stone throwing. (Who kept injecting the comical elements into the struggle?)

"You have to practice throwing stones on threshing floors." (Threshing floors—what a heroic world that word contains.) "Otherwise you cannot do it," one of my classmates from the Mesaoria would say. ("Unfortunately for you, there were no threshing floors in Wales, James.")

The boys from the villages were simply terrific stone throwers. As soon as they took one in their hands, you could see that a savage, primitive instinct came over them. They were no longer the gentle, shy village boys you knew, with large, innocent, curious eyes; they looked (this is not a literary affectation) as if the old phrase "to return with your shield or on it" had suddenly come to life inside of them, as if they had discovered an ancient inheritance within themselves. As if some ancient story was being repeated and, like the warriors of ancient Sparta, they were combing their hair quickly for battle. They weighed the stones (with what familiarity and precision each weighed the stone—no, not weighed, more like caressed it as if it were an old friend). "Get these city boys out of my way." He whispered something to the stone, aimed, and away it went like a homing pigeon to the roost. The little bodies completely vibrated, the little souls were entirely engaged; everything was put into the throw. (Take the discus thrower out of the Museum; replace it with a statue of the stone thrower.) They did not just throw stones, they threw their hearts (the hearts went off like homing pigeons too). Hearts drained of blood, tied up in knots, clenched like a fist. How could the English match them?

The rest of us now took second place. The initiative passed to these village boys. They arranged things, they contrived a strategy.

"To the opposite roof. Quick." (What a climbing of stairs. What a battle from roof to roof.)

"Get them!"

The English always had many wounded. We had more, especially students from the lower grades with fractured skulls, broken ribs, black eyes.

When the battle finally ended (because it often lasted several hours), breathless fathers and worried mothers appeared on the scene.

"Did you see my son?"

"Children, did you see my son?" (The voice was always changing.)

"Children, did you see my son?"

ONE DAY my brother Nikos came home with a bloody bandage sticking out from under his hat. He had been wounded by the soldiers and then crudely attended to in a house behind the Gymnasium. There was always a friendly house to be found to use as first aid stations, where the women would lovingly bend over us and tend our injuries. They did not ask (they knew) and did not reprimand us for fighting. The questions and reprimands began when we returned home.

"What can come of all this, son? What are you able to accomplish using stones?"

Nikos entered exhausted and weak, and threw himself in a chair. My mother was scared and screamed.

"Mother of God! My son!"

"Sssh," Stalo and I tried to quiet her.

We called the doctor, and he stitched Nikos's wound. He said that Nikos had lost a lot of blood and ordered him to stay home for a few days.

That evening my mother tried to give him advice, or rather a piece of her mind.

"Nikos, for the love of God, you are just unarmed children."

Our father interrupted her.

"This is no time for such talk. Let the boy rest."

I understood that my father's intrusion was a sign of approval and encouragement, and his attitude during the days Nikos had to stay home proved it. It appeared, however (or so I thought), that Nikos was more affected by my mother's fear and tears than my father's approbation (yes, really, by her fear and her tears, or so it seemed), because after he returned to school, he no longer joined us in our scuffles with the English. When I saw Nikos quietly slip away and leave as we gathered to attack, I tried to tell myself that he was making a sacrifice for the sake of our mother for whom he had special affection (Mother, what have you done to us? Nikos, have you forgotten already that "before mother and father," especially since you had no need for the "before father"). But in the end I rejected all these reasons.

No, no, it just can't be. (We had settled all these things between us long ago.)

I felt Nikos had fallen from the high regard, the high admiration, in which I had always held him. Younger brothers tend to have a boundless admiration for older brothers; they idolize them. And until his wound, Nikos had always been at the front, in the first rank of students (Did I talk earlier about the village boys? Forget whatever I said then).

"Our Nikos." (How we had worshipped him!)

THE CONCENTRATION CAMPS had been established in July, but our neighborhood was not seriously affected by them until September, when the milkman, Antonis, was taken to the Kokkinotrimithia camp. At first, his wife had no idea where they had taken him or what had happened to him. She nearly went out of her mind. Every day in tears she left her children (she had a whole nest of them) with neighbors so that she could run to the police and the military. They sent her from one department to another, from one interrogation center to another, from one city to another.

Where else could she go, where else could she ask? She came back drained in the evening (pale and strained, hardly human in appearance) and gathered her children from the neighbors.

"Let's go, my son" (you cannot simply say these special phrases. You need to capture them with a tape recorder).

She had no more tears left to cry by that time, and no voice left. The neighborhood is a wise, wonderful organism—no one has bothered to study it seriously until very recently, to examine its rules, its heart, its humanity. It understood (oh, how quickly it understood). It asked no questions (you know how discreet it is). It offered no consolation (it knows when an offer of consolation leads only to greater grief). The only thing it could offer was that the family would not be in need. It never neglected Antonis's family. This was a proud neighborhood. No philanthropic society, no government agency, could possibly compare with it. The neighborhood, as I have said, was like a living organism; it shared bread with itself, as it were, it gave bread so that bread could be put in its own mouth (sing a song about this neighborhood).

After an agonizing month, Antonis's wife was finally informed that her husband "was now detained in the Kokkinotrimithia camp." This was the usual wording, "was now." What did that "now" signify? It was like the "today" at Kyrenia—"you cannot testify today"—only, of course, worse. The letter went on to say that "unfortunately" (they really did put in that "unfortunately") it had been impossible to let her know earlier because of certain indispensable formalities. "You understand." (Yes, we certainly understood those formalities.) It said that she would be able to visit him at the camp when she received from him a card giving the day and time.

43

She cried for joy at the notification letter. He was alive. And despite its dreaded return address, and the hated signature at the bottom, she clutched it to her chest.

The pass arrived the very next day. On the day appointed for the visit, Antonis's wife combed her hair, dressed the kids in their Sunday clothes, packed the koulouria and sweets she had prepared (no Easter had ever had such elaborate cakes and sweets) and hurried to catch the very first bus of the day. She must have been up at midnight, if she slept at all. (Anticipation makes sleep even more difficult, more uncontrollable, than anxiety?)

She did not walk, she did not run, she flew, with the children chirping behind her.

"Give him our best," the neighborhood shouted. "Give him our love," the neighborhood said (the neighborhood knows so well how to converse in such circumstances). "Greetings. Tell him to be patient. And not to worry about the children." (You feel secure when a neighborhood promises.)

But she was not flying when she returned that evening, she drooped, her once wavy hair stuck to her head all askew, her once fluttering arms now stuck to her sides like she was an archaic statue. And behind her the children despondently dragged themselves along.

Now the neighborhood could ask, and it did.

"They have tortured him," she said. "They have disfigured him, they have made him a shadow of himself." She was frightened when she saw him. (She cried and the children cried.) And, you know, she added, he suddenly would lose himself and stare off strangely.

"Why was she crying?" the neighborhood asked. "It's all over now." It knew it was not over, but it was necessary, from experience it knew that it was necessary, to say that it was over. It knew only too well what they must have done to him, it knew what sort of recollection made him suddenly cut off his memory. It knew (we all knew) what sort of chains they have used on his bare back; what fists hit the stomach; what blood would be coughed up, how many times they would hold his head under water until he would lose consciousness; how they would tighten an iron band around his temples; how many nights they would prod him continually all night to prevent him from sleeping; how they would shine bright spotlights into his eyes during endless hours of interrogations until he wanted to beat his brains out against the wall to make an end of it. (To end it? And the children? Ah, yes, the children.)

(Perhaps someone should someday write the story of Antonis the milkman; and put in all the things I've left out; and say that he was a simple man, not very bright; and talk about his thoughts, his children (let their names be included), his pockets filled with peanuts every evening when he'd come home, his push-cart, his effort to make ends meet.)

THE DETAINMENT of Antonis the milkman had special significance for our house, because, after his wife, the next person to receive a "visiting card" from him was my father. I hastened to boast about this at school, which turned out to be a huge mistake when my father told us the next day that he would not be going.

What? He would not go? Now what did this mean? (What, in God's name, did this mean, Father?) I was confused. (Did he ask of you some enormous favor? Why, after all, should it even be considered a favor? He did you, he did our family, an honor by asking you to come. Why did you tell us about the Uprising of October and your speech for the boy who had died—"Dearly departed, the Pancyprian Gymnasium kneels reverently before you." Do you spurn him because he is a milkman? Bear in mind that, at this moment, he is better than you, better than all of us.)

I did not say all these things to him, of course, but I did ask him to explain. (Should I have waited for someone else to ask him—my mother, Stalo, or Nikos? No, I myself wanted to save our family's honor.)

"Father, why won't you go?"

"I can't. It would depress me too much."

(It would depress you too much? Why did you even bother to answer me? Why didn't you just tell me to mind my own business? Father, that wretched milkman must have been taken in by your passionate stories of the past. He must have been completely taken in, as, I have to say, were we all. Father, you were not worthy to receive a visitor's pass from the milkman, our home was not worthy to receive a visitor's pass from such a man.)

"I have already told the whole school about it, Father."

He did not answer. (Yes, but how can I even face the other children now, Father?)

Very soon, others from our neighborhood joined Antonis in detention, thousands from all over the island. As detention became a familiar part of life for me, the particular case of Antonis and my father's refusal to see him gradually lost any particular importance, in fact it lost any meaning at all. The time came when, from our suburb alone, four or five buses ran to the detention camps—to Kokkinotrimithia, to Pyla, to Mammari.

The buses for the camps left just like the ones that carried the crowds out to the village festivals, only without the red and white streamers, the songs, and the commotion. Although full of passengers, the camp buses were silent and eerily empty.

Visiting days became the most significant events for thousands of families.

"We will make a 'visit' tomorrow" (The island will remember that phrase for years to come. It is lodged as deeply and unchangeably in our memory as the words "Will we have rain this year?").

Everything else was set aside now, everything revolved around the visits; time itself revolved around them. And the day after a visit, people began to count the days until the next one; they started to arrange their lives around the next trip.

A moment ago, I mentioned festivals. There was a kind of festival atmosphere outside the camps. But it was a strange, glum festival, a festival from another world, from Hades; a festival of waiting—waiting for hours and hours through rain or fierce sun, with eyes glued to the big door that would open, with ears strained to hear it creaking open. There were, of course, cake stalls, lemonade stands, and ice cream vendors as at other festivals. But they too seemed like they were from another world; there was no crying of their wares, no conversation with the customers. ("Don't think that we come here simply to make a sale," their actions said. "We considered that a child gets thirsty, that a child gets bored, and you might not know what to do to calm him without a lemonade or ice cream.")

Later an Englishman would appear with the key.

"He is coming!" ("He is coming!" "He is coming!")

He held the key to a father, a brother, a husband, a child. But this key did not carry with it the promise of a touch or embrace. Only the eyes (only? Take out that "only"!), only the eyes (are you repeating it?) could reach those behind the barbed wire, feasting on the beloved faces, fixed sorrowfully on them without ever becoming unglued. The fingers were all that could attempt to get through the small holes in the wire. (Could that ever be a real substitute for a touch or a hug? Wasn't this an even older story?) And the talk would go on endlessly, and the hours would seem like moments.

"The bell? Not the bell so soon? The house is dark, my son. Our hearts are dark."

THE STRUGGLE kept growing, as I said (did I say it?) in intensity and breadth, so in October a new governor was sent to Cyprus (this time a military man). The English media trumpeted his appointment. They gave us details about his career and took pains to make us aware of the many colonial rebellions he had successfully suppressed (what a typically colonial word—"suppressed"). He took one look at us (as if to say, "Are you the ones?"). He had those pursed English lips that press together so tightly that they do not let in the cold, that English cold that makes the people there so distrustful and cunning. (What did we have to oppose those pursed, distrustful lips except for our trusting faces open to the sun and the spring? I don't know, I just don't know.)

Right behind him came the "red caps," as we later called them when we knew them better, and the commandos. And we certainly got to know them well. Even in England, they told us, people feared them.

"Here we will make them fear us!" we children said. (I have already warned you what a mistake it is to get into a war of words with children.)

And not only children (we still have not discussed where childhood begins and ends). The English, it appeared, had completely misjudged our resolve. They had not realized how intoxicated we were, how much of the romantic wine of great moments we had drunk, how at times the drunken heart can take charge of the head, a drunken heart that we experienced for the first time. We did not even know from where our determination originated. But our hearts no longer understood threats, they did not read the newspapers. They only reread over and over that first leaflet of Dighenis. Our hearts had taken that leaflet in and folded themselves around it ("with God's help").

We children (and perhaps the adults) did not fully understand what the governor's appointment meant. But the Organization knew, Dighenis knew that his presence foretold a grinding of teeth, that the real contest on the marble threshing floors was about to begin, that the battle of attrition was underway. On the next day, the leaflet said: "We will humiliate your commanders and your army!"

That leaflet brought warm tears to our eyes. It was our own thoughts and sentiments, precisely as we would have written them.

48

BUT THE FIST did not strike immediately. It dangled over us at first (the English know how to use such threats). Let's talk first ("I'll give you one last chance"). And they talked. With chilled hearts we followed these "negotiations" with the archbishop, and when they collapsed in March, we felt a kind of relief (not relief, joy, an enormous childish joy). (Hadn't they said that they would not "allow" our struggle to last for even one year?)

Now the fist could strike and it did. The archbishop and three "agitators" were hurriedly put on an airplane and exiled to the end of the earth (once more the same old tactics, once more the same knee-jerk reactions).

It seems that, hard as we tried, we didn't know the English well. (We didn't know this side of them, and who knew how many other sides they might have?) We were astonished.

"Did they send him into exile simply because he would not agree with them?"

The archbishop was one pillar of our admiration and love, and his arrest, news of which spread through the island like lightning, turned our world upside down. It fell upon the skin next to our hearts, it bored into us and shattered us. It was like reversing all the signs on the streets and roads, and forced us to reconsider, just as that first casualty had some months earlier (What first casualty? That first casualty meant nothing now).

At the news of the archbishop's exile, the stores closed immediately, the streets emptied in a second, and a heavy cloud of grief covered the city as the church bells chimed mournfully (I've explained I can only speak about Nicosia). They continued until dusk, resounding above the other funereal sounds, above the petrified figures, above the pervasive gloom, above the wailing laments of the women:

"May God cut off the hands that touched him."

The little children curled up at the feet of their mothers to ask what terrible thing had happened. Grandmothers began to spin the beginnings of a new tale (as they had in Constantinople), the first thread of a golden spindle of a new myth on the spinning wheel.

Grandmother ruminated over and over about the profound sense of foreboding of the archbishop on the night before he was seized (Where does her intuition come from?).

This premonition was a good element for the construction of a legend, just as at Constantinople, exactly as at Constantinople five centuries earlier. Later she would find other details for the story, like the letters that seamen passing the island of exile placed in bottles and consigned to the waves to deliver to the archbishop.

On the next day, we translated all of these things, the sorrows of the fathers and the laments of the mothers, into fierce collisions with the English soldiers. (What did you say about the Spartans and the arrows flying through the streets?) Our stones flew as never before, carrying a message of hate, a message of bottomless hate.

THE EXILE OF THE ARCHBISHOP was followed by an incredible wave of oppression. In the interrogation rooms of Omorphita (whose name, "beautiful place," they took and see what they made of it) of Xeros, of Platres. (Did the famous nightingales know who sang in their ravines! Did they know? They knew! That spring they did not make love, they did not sing in the ravines.) Fingernails were pulled out, backs burned with lighted candles, ribs broken, hair ripped out by the roots. And when a prisoner could take no more and died, they put a bullet in him and announced that he had been "killed while trying to escape." We knew what that phrase meant, and the English knew that we all knew, but they didn't care. Perhaps it was their strategy to let us know, since interrogators themselves readily admitted it and spread it around.

"You know (they always began with "you know"), if you don't talk, I can kill you and say that you were trying to escape?" (This was in the last phase of interrogation, of course. They began with promises, with piles of money on the table. They began with your wife, your children, your mother. (They were saying something about your children—what was it—or they were not saying anything about your children?) Later they would strap you to an iron bed (have any of these iron beds been preserved?) and dance upon your back with their boots on. They would hold your head underwater. (Have I mentioned these things?) They would put an iron crown around your head.)

They undressed the women and paraded them in front of the Turkish auxiliaries. They burnt their nipples with cigarettes, they placed hot eggs under their armpits.

Torture was hardly confined to the interrogation rooms. Across the entire island, especially in the villages where foreign journalists never went, the "red caps" tortured, killed, and demolished houses. Sometimes they forced suspects to dig holes ("I don't like that face"). The soldiers then threw the "suspects" into the holes and began to cover them with earth (remember the incident at Kyrenia).

"You will talk now?"
"I don't know anything."
More earth.
"You will talk now?"
"I don't know anything."

Never before had that Cypriot obstinacy been so evident, so impressive. That taciturn obstinacy that says "no" and leaves it at that. Which often does not even say no, but simply moves its head to signify the immovable and irrevocable negative. The English, to be sure, had their own kind of obstinacy (I have already told you about their pursed lips).

"Bloody fool" (the same old insult).

When the earth came up to their mouths, they passed out and the soldiers would grab them by the hair and pull them out of the hole. And then the whole process would begin again.

"Come on! Speak up!"

"I don't know anything."

Broken, incoherent words from the labored breathing (write that "I don't know anything" on the top of the Pentadactylos. You have seen the Pentadactylos Mountains bend their peaks upwards to make that same "no"? Surely the suspect was inspired by those mountains?).

In the coastal regions, the English used other tactics. They bound the hands of a suspect and towed him in the water behind a boat. When the man sank, they pulled him out and made him cough up the water he had swallowed. Then they threw him back in the sea.

"Come on! Speak up!"

"I don't know anything." (Write that "I don't know" on the top of the Troodos.)

In May we had the first executions. Two boys, one twenty and the other twenty-two, Michael and Andreas. I have to tell you their names, they are an important part of the story, but there is no need for the mention of last names. Michael and Andreas. They stare out from the photographs in the newspapers with a surprised look. They seem younger than their years, their broad, fresh smiles suggest an age of fifteen. The photos suggest that they have not taken in what has happened to them (have I repeated this phrase?).

Michael managed to make notations in his Bible, worn out from reading with several torn pages and a broken binding, about the torture they had endured in jail. (Leave his mother in the dark about this. Don't tell her what those barely legible little marks say. Don't tell her about the mock executions that the commandos made each day outside their cells.)

"Kih" (the sound of a knife slicing across a throat).

The boys closed their eyes. They held their hands to their ears so they would not have to listen.

"*Eh you, kih.*"

On the night before the hanging the city of Nicosia was unable to sleep. The houses, the city walls, and the people were tossing and turning with sleeplessness. From early in the evening all traffic had been forbidden and military vehicles patrolled the city continuously as if they had no plan, no aim, not even a steering wheel, just like ants who disperse in all directions at once or like the toy electric cars at a carnival. The drivers had a strange triumphant look on their faces, an ill-omened look of triumph because wasn't this the last hope left for them? What hesitations did all that frenetic movement try to disperse, what doubts?

In the areas around the prison, a crowd was hidden in the yards of the houses. There was a person behind every column, every fountain, every tree, every rose bush. Some were standing, some sitting, others lying flat upon the ground. They listened mute, dumbfounded, holding their breath.

When, a little after midnight, they brought the two boys from their cells (everyone knew they were taken out; they saw them without seeing them, they touched them and caressed their hair), they (Michael and Andreas) began to sing the Greek National Anthem. (Where are you taking Michael and Andreas at such an hour? Why have you awakened the boys so early?)

Like whispers, like the falling of dry leaves (I don't know how to describe it exactly) their interrupted, faint voices traveled through the May night (one star grabbed half a note, another half a note, the trees recorded another syllable in their roots, so the earth will have it when she needs it. Why did you make that night so beautiful, God? Why did they choose a such a night? Could they rob them of their remaining years on such a night? Could Spring be slaughtered so? Could the mirror be shattered?).

"I know you by the sharp blade of your terrifying sword . . . " (The first words of the Greek anthem came through).

The crowd outside the prison kneeled in tears. Hearts pounded, heads throbbed, women fainted. And again:

"I know you by the form you made . . . "

No, not quite like the sound of falling of dry leaves now. Suddenly the voices of a hundred jailed men joined the two weak voices and the song thundered in the air, mingled with the memories of the klephts of the Morea, and the thick eyebrows of Kolokotronis.

"Sprung from Grecian bones scattered . . . "

The kneeling neighborhoods outside the walls whispered the words, they did so differently, as if at prayer (God must have wondered who was praying with a martial song). The sounds and silence of the night kept time with the singers.

Later came the dramatic cries of encouragement from the other prisoners.

"Courage boys!"

"Courage Andreas!" (the name of the youngest one always came first).

"Courage Michael!"

"Long live Greece."

The cheers (they were all cheers) traveled through the quiet night. The two boys were only twenty and twenty-two. And the gentle May night allowed the cheers to pass. It's a good thing that those cheers did not become a song bathed in the smell and breath of the blossoming oranges. The sound went through the heart of Nicosia, rolling up over the walls, across the moat.

And again to Andreas. (Who calls Andreas?)

"Courage, my Andreas" (Why "My Andreas" now? What stories, what history, are contained in that pronoun? It was not necessary to appeal to the boy's courage, it was not necessary to bolster his resolve.)

"Don't be afraid!"

Afraid? Who is afraid? Age flowed into them in a second (it came in a second); the boys of twenty and twenty-two years no longer had an innocent, surprised look (surprise is a fearful thing). They climbed the gallows as men, kissing their Bibles at the bottom of the steps, with the National Anthem on their lips. They sang it hoarsely (no, they did not sing it; they forged and reforged it) as the rope was put tightly around their necks, they sang it until their voices were cut off at their last syllable (no, the last syllable was not their own, but simply the vibrations of their vocal chords when further instructions from the brain had been cut off).

When the voices of the boys died out, when the two red lights on the gallows went out with them (what is the meaning of these two red lights, what purpose did they have?)

a complete silence filled the prison. The other prisoners kneeled. Everything was buried under a great weight, crushed under a great burden, pressed and squeezed. The yards of the houses were filled with groans. There was a groan behind every column, behind every fountain, behind every tree, behind every rose bush.

Two minutes passed. Five minutes. Two centuries. Five centuries: deaf, inexorable, empty, drained. And suddenly from a cell (like a fanciful, dramatic counterpoint) a rousing voice shouted (someone else, not the one who had called to Andreas):

"Long live Greece!"

What? What did the voice say? You turn around for a second to look. No, no, it was not the time for such cheers. And you slowly turn back, deflated. Even the crystalline night of May returns (could it save the betrayed Spring—yes, but no, no!).

Again came the cry of the voice (Who was it who knew what happened and still insisted?):

"Long live Greece!"

You turn again. And . . . (I'll give you a half second to think about it, a half second to put aside doubt. You who called to Andreas, I give you half a second. Night, I give you half a second).

"Long live Greece!" The voices of all the prisoners shouted.

And then, before they could change their minds, to prevent any further hesitation, more martial songs and again the Greek National Anthem.

"I know you by the sharp blade of your terrifying sword . . . " (Just seconds ago, Michael had sung it, and also Andreas).

The martial songs continued until morning in order to encompass the gallows, to cover the wound of the night, to fill the wound of Spring, so that the orange flowers could not enclose any memories when they folded.

At breakfast time, the guard (what could he have been thinking?) asked whether the prisoners wanted to eat. The men were angry.

"Why do you ask?"

"Perhaps—what do I know . . ."

"You don't know? Ask your bosses."

AND IT REALLY WAS A QUESTION that the jailer needed to ask his superiors. For they would have to prepare for a renewed commitment, an animosity several levels deeper than when the revolution started, a reinvigorated purpose.

"So this, then, is what the English are really like."

Yes, this was what they were like. What did you think? Didn't you realize that already without really admitting it? Let Greece still believe in England (and Greece really did seem to still believe in England. Perhaps, I don't know, Greece believed in her until the very end. We, since it was Greece, would find ways to forgive her):

"It is because she never considered them as enemies."

Hatred of England? In our house, I should tell you, Eleftherios Venizelos, the great Greek Prime Minister during the first part of this century, was a legendary hero. Venizelism was a family tradition. Before we learned the Greek National Anthem, we knew the Cretan "Song of the Son of Psiliroti."

"Without this song there would be no National Anthem," our grandfather told us, our father told us, and we, in turn, echoed it too.

We knew everything about Venizelos, the details of his life and activities, the anecdotes about him and his political accomplishments. We heard them around the fire during the endless nights of winter. Not from my grandmother; she was too caught up in her world of fairly tales and princes. The stories of Venizelos required a voice of plain unadulterated truth, they needed the voice of my grandfather or father.

Venizelos was like a spirit in our household, built somehow into the foundation like a household spirit or the big black snake in the garden. But his status was challenged by the revolution. His portrait in the living room was knocked a bit off-center by it. After the first hangings we came to hate him. (There was no room left for our hate to expand with the second and third hangings.) Yes, yes to hate him. Funny now, but it was true. Venizelos, at a different time, in different circumstances had been a stalwart friend of the English, their unshakable ally. So we all grew to hate him—father, mother, and the children (especially the children). The house deserted him. We never let him back in.

The English responded to the increased activity after the hanging (to their dead and wounded, which they had every day in the mountains, on the coasts, and in the cities) with a new wave of oppression. (Multiply all that I have said on this subject.) Their losses (losses caused by a handful of men, this was even more unendurable) so stunned and humiliated them, they threw off all of their humanitarian pretenses. They ignored the alliances with and public opinion of both Europe and America. Did public opinion exist? Did Europe or America exist? Really, what did public opinion in Europe or America, or the UN, or the Human Rights Commission, or the representative of the Red Cross, or the British Labour Party, or any of our other "friends" do for us? We became fed up with all of them, fed up with everything. Just leave us alone.

We children, entering a new phase in the struggle with growing zeal, chose not to discuss the mounting British losses in order to consider privately among ourselves in the middle of the night (privately? No, with a thousand voices) on what for us was a more momentous issue, the disappearance of the governor from the streets of Nicosia. (Children have strange antennae about things, but they are not always wrong.) The despised armored car, with its escort of military vehicles in front and behind, no longer annoyed us; that ugly, unbearable, black car no longer blemished our streets. The governor only traveled by helicopter now. (How ugly and awkward they are. What do they remind you of, these helicopters?)

We reveled in this new turn of events, and joked with one another:

"Well, we lost our friend."

And our feeling of triumph grew nearly immeasurable when a bomb was discovered beneath the governor's bed. We passed many nights contemplating this news, we hardly were able to believe it.

A bomb in his bed? This was really something else. (It was a long time after that we heard how the bomb was smuggled into the Government house: a small bit of powder each day, a small bit of iron each day, right under the noses of the three lines of guards and security men.)

After the executions of the two boys, all of us felt a visceral hatred for the governor. Even the simple old women of the villages spat whenever they saw a helicopter. They would take the black scarves from their faces and curse because they thought that the governor was inside every helicopter.

"May the curse of God be upon you, and may I see you dead!"

WHILE THE STRUGGLE reached its peak, something odd happened in our home. It was, in fact, hardly a home at all anymore. We had almost disintegrated as a domestic unit. It was as if we had suddenly transformed into strangers, each with his or her own separate life, with his or her own thoughts, own worries, and own associations. My father's schedule changed, so did Nikos's and Stalo's; the routine of the house had altered. We no longer sat in the evenings to discuss the struggle. We did not want to anymore, or did not have time, or did not have the heart (could this be possible?). Dialogues ceased, there were only monologues, private, hidden, secret monologues.

Did I say the home was "odd"? That's curious. Why "odd"? These days were so earth shattering for us that you knew that no one could help you comprehend them. (Not even father? No, not even father.) We knew that we had to come to grips with it individually, to sort it out alone, to find counsel and direction from within ourselves. Dialogues were for other circumstances. Now was the time for intimate whispering, private conspiracy, a concentrated collusion with the Mycenaean inheritance that lurked inside of us, with remnants of a heritage four thousand years old.

"What happens when they hang young Evagoras?"

"What happens when you are a handful and they are millions?"

Only that Mycenaean ancestry could answer. That held the strings which controlled our brains.

There was no one left in our house but my mother and myself; my mother in her desperate effort to prevent the total disintegration of the home, and I from necessity. I say "from necessity" because I did not want to be at home, I did not want to talk with my mother, I was continually undermining her attempts to keep total annihilation at bay, and I struggled to find a way to break free like the others. (Mother, don't wait for me at the usual time. Don't talk to me in the evenings, Mother, I have more important conversations, more pressing accounts, to make with myself.)

I said that I was struggling to break free because it was not easy to enroll in the Organization ("I swear in the name of the Holy Trinity that I shall work with all my strength for the liberation of Cyprus from the British yoke, even if I have to sacrifice my life").

I tried to find someone carrying a gun, or throwing a bomb, or distributing leaflets, so I could run right up to him ("Take me").

I begged Nikos (even though I was angry about his behavior when the students demonstrated). I begged Stalo.

They didn't know anything about it.

They knew nothing? Maybe Nikos didn't (although in my despair his denial seemed less and less plausible), but something smelled very suspicious about Stalo's answer. I began to spy on her. (My stubbornness, after a while, seemed to become an end in itself.)

I had observed the appearance of a new set of severe, hard-looking girlfriends, her sudden exits, her curious behavior. Slowly, I convinced myself that Stalo was my last hope and I stuck to her like glue. I watched her every move, I tried to eavesdrop on her conversations with her friends, I searched her bags and purse. For a long time I never came across anything. I failed for quite a while, but I never gave up. How could I give up when I had no other chance of success? (You do not easily abandon your last hope.)

Then I discovered them. One day in a drawer I discovered them carefully hidden between books and papers. A batch of freshly printed leaflets with the signature "EOKA, the leader Dighenis."

They stared up at me from their hiding place as if they were frightened to be discovered. They stared up at me as I grinned broadly and put my hand down to caress them. What a touch that was, what a caress! How did they manage to appear to change color, from the off-white of leaflet paper to blue, red, and yellow? How did they manage to grow petals like roses and daisies? I held them against my heart.

"Finally!"

I sat down to wait impatiently for Stalo to return (Impatiently? My heart beat violently and I gasped for breath).

She came in, sweating, excited, off her guard. Her glance took me in. ("What's the matter with you?")

("What's wrong with me? Just get your breath back first, and you'll see.")

("Come on, tell me.")

("Listen here, don't speak to me like that, not today.")

I asked her if she had seen the new leaflet. I asked her slowly, in those round, rough, unique Cypriot syllables inherited from Byzantium.

"No, not yet." (Stalo said "No"!)

A pause.

"The one with the battle at Soli, Stalo" (those same Cypriot syllables, and at the end, a quiet fall in "Stalo"). As an anchor falls into the sea, that is how I sent her name into the air, with a downward splash to fix firmly on the bottom.

"I haven't seen it yet. What do you want?" ("Don't ask me what I want like that, not today.")

Immediately, without pause, I emitted a single syllable. "Bah!"

She was surprised. ("Don't look at me like that, Stalo. I am ready.")

She thought a while.

"So you haven't seen it then?" ("I told you that I am ready, Stalo.")

She sensed some danger (once again she pondered a bit). She regained her composure.

"So what if I haven't seen it!" (That "so what" you repeat in jest will not save you now, Stalo.) "Do you know what's in it or not?"

"What does it say?" she asks. Does she hand them out without even reading them?

"What's that? What did you say?" (A mixture of surprise and challenge. Who had taught her such responses?)

I said, did she hand them out without reading them?

"What do you mean?" (Stalo asks what I meant.)

"You have a bunch of them in your drawer, Stalo."

She stood before me with her eyes popped open. Had I been searching her drawers? Yes, I admitted, I searched them.

She was angry. She began to scream at me and raise her voice.

(These are not answers, Stalo.)

(They are answers.)

The leaflets weren't hers, she replied.

"Bah, whose are they then?"

A girlfriend's.

60

I knew that I would not get anywhere by making her angrier, so I went right to my point and changed my tone to one of pleading.

"I want to join up, Stalo." (As if I read it off a page. As if someone else were saying it.)

She did not respect my tactic, and became bolder.

"The same old thing?"

"Tell your friend."

Did I really think it's that easy?

She said "Leave me alone." That was too much. Did she have any idea of what she was asking me to give up? Did she think I had watched so diligently for so long to be put off by one "No"? Was she aware of how I had worked to find those pamphlets, how I had squeezed them to my breast? In what corner of my mind could I put them that I would be able to forget about them now?

I looked for a silent confirmation of that "Leave me alone," and I saw it in her eyes ("Do you insist?"), exactly as it had been said at first, without any retreat or concession.

"Then I will have to tell father," I said, playing my final card.

"Tell him what!"

I gave her an angry look, and she returned it, more than returned it. What a look it was; wherever had she learned to make a look like that?

"Tell him!"

(Tell him? If you look at me like that, then, all right, Stalo, the leaflets are not yours. But that look is now yours. And it is the same, exactly the same look as the one on the faces of your companions (your companions, you hear?) in the newspapers after they were seized. That look—have I described it before?—came straight out of the history books (history exaggerates, of course) and schoolbooks (schoolbooks romanticize); somehow during the struggle those old heroes managed to look out at us not from a distance, as in years before, but from close by, in the present tense.)

If I had not been completely sure (from that look alone) that Stalo belonged to the Organization, I would have tried to pull her hair. But how can I even touch it now?

And, of course, I never said anything to father. I got very depressed (as only children can) because our family's good name depended only upon a girl.

IT DID NOT TAKE LONG for me to realize (despite my initial reaction), that even a girl was able to be a worthy representative of any house. So many girls hid hand grenades in their purses and pistols in their blouses. Aside from that, I soon found out that Stalo was not the only member of our household in the Organization. Nikos did not come home one evening. The clock struck seven, eight, nine, and still he did not appear. We were all afraid, and we four sat together as if we might be better able to face the suspected disaster (no time now for monologues or communion with the Mycenaean ancestry). We hung with anticipation for a knock on the door. Only my father absent-mindedly repeated every so often the same, monotonous sentences, as if in answer to his own, and to our, unspoken questions.

"Something has delayed him. He will come."

I was lost. Nikos, too? I stared fixedly and questioningly at Stalo, but she would not meet my gaze. This was not normal. Why wouldn't she look at me? I felt like shouting, "Father, Mother, Stalo must know something," but I held my tongue.

Time passed. It passed with the same monotonous reassuring sentences of my father, but they were a bit weaker now, there was a slight crack in the voice.

"Something has delayed him. He will come."

We did not answer him, we did not question him, we did not even listen any more. How could we listen? Perhaps my father did not even hear himself speak either, perhaps he was not aware that he was saying anything. The phrase echoed like empty words of consolation, so obviously empty that no reply is required, you just receive them with a slight, anemic smile (Yes, all right).

After eleven, my mother could not control herself any longer and began to cry. Stalo and I cried along with her. My father did nothing to stop the outburst. How could he have stopped it? Why would he try when he was on the verge of tears himself? He gave in. He abandoned his "something has delayed him" (it was completely useless now if it had ever really been of any use). He was bent over and lighting cigarette after cigarette.

At times, one of us would say,

"Quiet, I hear footsteps."

There would be movement, concentration, a holding of breath, a spark of hope. Later again a profound sinking (very deep now) of spirits:

"No, it was nothing."

"Can we call the police?" my mother timidly asked.

We did not bother to answer her. What could we say to such a suggestion?

"I don't believe Nikos is mixed up in anything," I said, in a monotone. "I am sure."

They did not answer me. It was as if I had not spoken, as if they had not heard. They did not even turn to look at me, did not even raise an eyebrow to my "I am sure."

Again the terrible silence. And again the stifled weeping of my mother. We were floundering below the surface, fumbling blindly around in the darkness. At twelve, a car suddenly stopped in front of our house. We all sprang up.

"Holy Virgin," my mother cried.

We all repeated her "Holy Virgin" in our souls. (Holy Virgin, our Nikos?)

Loud knocks rang out upon our front door.

"I'll answer it," my father said.

It was not the voice of my father however; it was a strange voice that suddenly echoed harshly and imperiously through the house. It struck me as a voice for military orders. I felt (not felt, but trembled) just as I had when I saw that look of Stalo's after I discovered her pamphlets.

We all made to follow him to the door, but he fixed us with such a stare that we remained nailed to our places. "I'll answer it," he repeated. (No, this was not father.)

A tall English officer entered with five soldiers. They were looking for Nikos.

Looking for Nikos? Immediately our tears dried up, our eyes could see again. All of a sudden we could hear things clearly.

"He hasn't come home yet," my father answered.

They put us all in one room in order to search the house.

We embraced and wept for joy, all of us, including father. We squeezed each other's hands silently.

"Only don't let him come home now."

"He won't come."

And again the squeezing of hands.

They ransacked the house for a long time, then they said they would wait for him. Three remained behind and two left. We heard the car go a ways down the street and stop. It appeared they would wait for him in the yard. They put out all the lights in the house, and sat silently and patiently through the night. And we sat up with them.

But they waited in vain. Nikos never came home. At dawn, they left. (How sweet that morning was. What a relief when the door finally closed behind them.)

We sat together to talk, to talk about the anxiety that had ended and the anxiety that had just begun. Mother asked the questions (we let her have this role, it was the mother's role), and the rest of us answered her. How readily we supplied the answers, as if we did not all have the same questions ("Really, how can you ask such a question, Mother?" But she was his mother and she dared to ask them). Later the neighborhood came to satisfy its ignorant curiosity about the visit from the soldiers, and behind them the journalists.

The next day, a photograph of Nikos was in all of the newspapers, smiling, his schoolboy's cap slightly askew on his forehead. My mother kissed it as if she had never seen the picture before, as if she herself had not given it to the press ("I will give you the best one"). And in truth it was not the same photograph any longer. The cap seemed different somehow, so was the smile. And the look was the look I had seen on Stalo, on my father—that look taken from history and the schoolbooks.

A LARGE PART of our home left with Nikos. How we all missed him. His absence weighed heavily upon us; smiles no longer graced the faces of my parents, and if, on occasion, Stalo or I formed one, it felt artificial and contrived, as if we had no right to smile.

And we feared the worst.

"A battle? Where?"

"They killed some of ours? Who, does it say?"

"Do they give the names of the captured?"

That "who" tortured us. We lived in a continual state of agony. We knew that we should not expect a message from Nikos; we knew that the only way we would know anything about him was if he was killed or captured.

The loss of Nikos brought our house together again; the family had, as I said earlier, been close to dissolving. But while our constant anxiety about Nikos managed to tie us together again, it was an entirely different kind of unit than before. Could our "family" now exist without Nikos? Did I call it a "unit"? No, it was not really a unit. In truth, we moved even further apart (forgive the continual contradictions) because the change that I referred to earlier had now been completed. Father, mother, Stalo, and I, each of us was a new person now. And we experienced wide swings of mood, individually and together. At certain moments we thought that we had great public responsibilities, that our house was involved in the making of history, that we had to defend and uphold the heroism of our Nikos (and how that "our" formed on our lips). Nikos had marched out in front and we, it seemed, had to fall in behind—just like the mother who, after her only son had been hanged, waved her handkerchief to the crowd at his funeral with her husband smiling beside her. We, like the others, had clapped wildly at her patriotic gesture. But at other moments, we became private human beings again—a father, a mother, a sister, a brother. We were afraid, and we leaped with terror from our beds at the hoot of an owl in the middle of the night. How is it that, even in deepest sleep, no matter how softly it sounds, the hoot of an owl can come through the night to disturb one? (How is it that it can penetrate the subconscious? What kinds of ill omens, according to the folk tales, does it carry?)

"Mother, did you hear it?"

"You should be ashamed of yourself for believing in such things," father said.

Yes, but we sensed that he too was afraid. (Everything scared us now, in such circumstances you reexamine things, you give credence to beliefs you thought that you had grown beyond.)

The people in the neighborhood of Ayios Dometios would point us out, for when Nikos disappeared there were still only a few families that had one of their own in the mountains. In a short time, however, that had no particular significance and they all lost interest.

"Their son is 'wanted'!"

In school (on the few days when we actually went to class) my fellow pupils looked at me with awe. (His brother is "wanted"!) Everyone wanted to be my friend, to buy me a lemonade or a sweet (if, that is, the shopkeeper would take their money after he saw me with them).

And my teachers treated me differently as well. ("Yes, my boy." I understood that the sweet way they would say "my boy" was for Nikos, not for me.)

I tried to tell my mother about all this, to console her with it, but I never managed to do it. How could I have succeeded? What meaning did any of these things have when the central fact of all our lives was that Nikos was gone?

IN AUGUST, the English hanged three other boys, and in September another three. Each time, Nicosia was unable to sleep the night before. The houses, walls, and people tossed and turned with restlessness, the military vehicles traversed the city (like ants released from a box), a crowd knelt in the area outside the prisons, and the voices from the cells sang the Greek Anthem. Then came the hopelessness, the silence, finally broken by the cry ("Long Live Greece!").

(Iacovos did not sing the Greek Anthem on the way to the gallows, but a religious hymn. He had a calm, high, sweet voice, one of the sweetest voices that had ever praised God.)

Then came the retaliatory attacks by the Organization, and the desperate attempts of the English to benefit from the terror of the gallows.

It was after these hangings that the English instituted punitive *curfews*. (I use the English word because it is weighed down with such pain, blood, and hurt, that it's not possible to find an equivalent to the cursed thing in Greek.) As soon as an "incident" occurred (they always referred to them as "incidents"), they imposed a curfew (I'm only speaking about Nicosia of course). A daring attack in Ledra Street in Nicosia —called "murder mile" by the English—was an "incident," an ambush in Royiatiko was an incident, as was an unexpected skirmish where the gun had been concealed under a rain coat, or a bomb thrown through the door of a restaurant or dropped from a roof onto a passing jeep or truck. The curfew could last several days and for poor families who had little in their cupboards and no income except the daily wages of a father or brother it was a real hardship. When the curfews became regular events, the English would let the women go out for one or two hours to shop for food, but there were often so few provisions in the stores and so great a crowd of customers that some people found nothing to buy. Those who had no money had to run (if you could have seen with what anxiety they ran) to beg a loan from a relative or friend ("Just a few pounds for the children's sake") and then run again to purchase whatever they could find before the two hours was up.

After a while, shipments of food had to be sent from all over the island. And it was not only hunger that the lower classes had to endure, but thirst as well. Many homes in Nicosia got their water from public taps, and how could they all manage to draw what they needed in the space of two hours?

And the strain of the curfew did not end with hunger and thirst. There was a nagging nervousness that affected everyone equally. It was a strain on the nerves similar at times to a breakdown. What, people would ask themselves, will I do if my child suddenly becomes sick during a curfew and I can't get a doctor or medicine? What if my pregnant wife needs attention? A thousand such cares ate at the mind.

The strain was greatest in downtown Nicosia inside the walled part of the city (look how quickly it accumulates, see what happens when it builds up). There the streets were narrow, and the houses were glued to each other, and neighbors made irritable by confinement would needlessly argue. In suburbs like ours, where the houses were set apart and each had its own garden, the pressure was a bit less. And the curfew in the suburbs was also less severe because their size and expanse made it difficult to patrol them as rigorously.

It was in the suburbs that the kites first appeared. During the curfews, you could see hundreds of kites in the air, flown not only by children but also by grown men and women. I don't know how it started, or if there was a reason behind it. Were they meant to be some comic relief in a period of stress, or did they have a deeper significance? Did a childish prank first send them into the air (to confuse us even more, and to make it impossible to discover when childhood begins and ends?), or some subconscious desire? (I don't know if there is not a common subconscious for adults and children, if the subconscious ages like a person—why should it? Why couldn't it age in reverse, and get younger as the body gets older?) Were the kites, as some foreign journalists suggested, a desperate attempt to escape from the curfew, so desperate as to be almost laughable? Or was it just playing? You could see adults, even old women in black, enjoying their kites dancing in the sky and you feared that all of Nicosia had gone mad. Whatever the cause, the kites from the suburbs arrived over the houses within the walls of Nicosia and brought support and encouragement. The kites maintained contact between people separated by the curfew (it seems a bit romantic and at the same time contrived, no?). Who knows for whom the old woman's kite was sent up? The kites were mostly blue and white. They would make their daily walk over the prison walls and offer greetings; they carried our souls above the gallows. (No, now that I think about it, it was surely not a childish prank at all. I ought never to have suggested such a thing.)

The kites of the English, for they joined in, were simply child's play. The English had to participate, to join that sky filled with Cypriot kites, when their children became jealous, when their children cried and stamped their feet. "Daddy, I want a kite, too." Was this the reason that the English never dared forbid the kites, they were afraid to face the wrath of their own children? These brave servants of the Queen were not only forced to make kites for their children, but, many times, were forced to fly them as well. ("Daddy, I can't. I can't make it stay up.") Adding to the ridiculousness, during the worst of the emergency measures, they flew their children's kites while armed, a kite string in one hand and a sten gun or pistol ready in the other!

(The kites of the English, I must tell you, were not like ours, but similar to the ones they had known as children back in Brighton or Bodmin. In the Cypriot sky, among our blue and white kites, those foreign kites seemed like some strange migratory birds.)

DURING THE CURFEW, we had an "incident" in our neighborhood. (Don't look for anything more specific, leave it simply as an "incident." Leave it just as it is.) I would be unfair to those involved if I failed to mention it, and why should I want to be unfair to anyone now? It was just a small incident, but for half a second it was able to break the terrible ring of hatred, an incident that lodged itself, seared itself, in one's memory.

We were enduring, I remember, the third week of a ruthless curfew that (for the first time) they tried to impose as strictly upon the suburbs as those in the city. Continual, relentless patrols shut everyone in their houses. Doors didn't open and close, voices did not break the quiet in the street, kites did not even venture out. Even the English children disappeared from view and with them their odd triangular birds.

The smallest children, who felt the confinement the most, glued their faces to the windows and watched the sun beckon them out to play, the street call out to them ("We can't today," their faces answered sadly). Every window in every house seemed to have little faces in them, the noses pressed up against the glass (as closely as possible) the chins and eyebrows flattened against the glass. Then, for just a second, a door suddenly opened and a ball came rolling out. Who knows what impatient little hand sent that ball out into the street, what childish tantrum? (No, let's imagine that the ball was thrown out to take in a little sun, to have a little game beyond the closed confines of the house.)

(Game? How could it have a game with no children? It rolled alone in the deserted street. Someone take a picture of that ball rolling in the deserted street! Stage it in the theater!) Not alone, exactly. It carried the eyes of all those faces pressed to the glass with it. It rolled down the street until it met an English patrol, and one of them bent down to pick it up. A tall Englishman raised it up, looked at the windows around him, and saw the faces of the children. They gazed at him intently, wide-eyed, until in his mind they began to whirl together into one large pair of blue eyes. He turned to the left and to the right, asking with hand gestures.

"Is it yours?"

No, he can't concentrate on his question. His mind had flown elsewhere, and his hand stays extended with the ball in the air. What would he ask? That pair of eyes, are they Freddy's eyes? ("Daddy, Daddy!" Who is calling "Daddy?")

70

All of these homes have become his home, they are all his home back in Bodmin.

He throws the ball gently behind the large Christmas tree. No, he does not throw it, he carefully places it down.

"There!" (Who could reproduce that "There" on a page, who could analyze what it means, all that it says?)

I don't know now, as I read what I have written, if the incident with the ball is really related to what I was going to tell you about, whether I have mixed things up and given it more importance than it really had—just a simple parenthesis in the atmosphere of despair during the curfews.

For I had not wanted to talk about children, but about flowers. About the parched flowers that, for many days, gloomily looked at us from the yard and begged for a little water. Flowers just don't understand; you can't explain things like a curfew to them. Although it is really a different case, we also at crucial moments do not understand, and watch and wait while a tragedy occurs before our eyes and simply cannot take it in ("no, no, we simply cannot understand how this can happen"). From the window, we could see the flowers droop and wither. One of our neighbors could not endure the pleas of his cherished flowers any longer. Ignoring the curfew, he went out to water them. (Who knows how many nights those dying flowers had troubled him with sleeplessness, what they had been saying to him in his dreams?)

"For the love of God, are you thinking about the flowers now," his wife yelled at him, but he did not listen and he did not stop. He rushed like a madman to the tap, fastened the hose, and began watering. His face shined. It was not simply water that he put on those flowers, but his own heart. (Have I used this expression once too often? I will be careful from now on.)

At such moments, reality always lies in wait for us. At such moments, a patrol just has to come down the street (in this it resembles poetry, doesn't it?). And one came. They entered the yard, they looked him over with their weapons ready, then they put him up against the wall with his hands up. His terrified wife was screaming inside the house, the children were crying at the top of their lungs.

"What are you doing?"

"Watering the flowers. They are dying."

71

They looked him over again. They thought for a moment. Perhaps they were aware of the cries coming from the house. They decided to show him some mercy.

"Don't do that again. Get in."

And they gave him a push toward the house.

What? Go inside? Shut off the water and go inside? How could he shut off the water just as the first drops were beginning to reach the roots of the plants? Would it not be a crime? It could not be possible that men would make him do such a thing.

He did not move at the shoves. He refused to leave on his own accord. He stood his ground.

"I can't," he said. "They'll die. Look at them. *Look*" (that *"look"* had a sound like a dry rasp).

Look at them? But he needed no other defense, no other words. "Look at them." (It had a sound, that "Look at them" (a sharp accentuation—not a sharp one, really, but a long one).) (Don't be afraid of a double parentheses. What is a double parentheses or two in life?)

And they looked. The officer turned his head and looked. He saw the dying carnations, tulips, and pansies. He stooped over them as if trying to somehow make them come upright without bending down, it was difficult for him to bend down on duty in front of his men. He walked a few steps among the withering little lives. And suddenly, just like the soldier with the ball, he was transported to the bright flowers and happy voices of Wales. He breathed in those familiar voices, those comforting voices. He cast a glance back at his companions to see the effect of the scene on them. And little by little he became less timid, for he saw that within them Wales, or Lancashire, or Scotland was speaking.

The voice from the flowers called names, it continually whispered the names in their ears, and with it a vision of a small hand plucking a rose, a small hand gathering jasmine (Who was that calling *Daddy*?).

He looked again at his company (in many circumstances they communicated without words: "Ready?" "Yes, we are ready"). But a final moment of hesitation tried to intervene. However the voice kept calling the names. Wales was now dancing inside of him, Wales was crawling in the ground in front of him. ("Are we ready?" His look asked again. "We're ready. We told you before.")

72

"All right, we'll do it. You get in."
We will water them, they said.
What? ("We told you, we'll water them. Get inside.")
And they watered them. They left their guns on the ground. They rolled up their sleeves (they left Cyprus, they rolled up their sleeves in Wales) and watered the thirsty flowers. Because of the slow trickle of the hose, it took a whole hour for them to finish, but who keeps track of time when one is back in Wales?

I HAVE MENTIONED the part of Nicosia within the old Venetian walls. It was the most densely populated area of the city, with Greek, Turkish, and Frankish quarters (each a completely different world). Within a few steps of one another were churches, mosques, covered Venetian balconies, the square of Serai where the Turkish Pasha's palace had stood, the carved arches of the fountains in Royiatiko, and drooping, neglected palms. It was honeycombed with narrow streets filled with sounds of blacksmiths and coppersmiths, and through the doors of their shops one could see the goldsmiths laboring at their trade. At certain points, the small lanes suddenly met the central commercial arteries lined with modern stores.

Around the old city ran a half-ruined Venetian fortification wall that, in the years of my early childhood, I remember was filled with the nests of starlings. During springtime, the white and yellow daisies climbed these walls as if they were thousands of soldiers competing to see who could be the first to plant his standard on the parapet beside the Turkish cannon.

The daisies let out little cries when blown against the wall by the spring wind, and the sound muted the twitter of the swallows. In front of the walls was a moat, filled, in past years, with tall eucalyptus trees. In the evening they were covered with crows, whose evil-omened shrieks frightened us. Now, however, the moat has become a park. Most of the eucalyptus trees have been cut down and the crows have left.

Beyond the walls the new city of Nicosia began, free from the memory of conquerors, completely Greek, well-built, clean, wrapped in a green smile. New and separate, but intimately linked to the old because it contained the large stores, the government buildings, the schools, and the hospitals. So the sudden (and they were always sudden) curfews in the walled city, the "closing of the walls," caused serious concern for however many thousands who lived outside. Usually the walls would close before the sirens had started to wail. As soon as news of an incident spread—and it spread like lightning ("Three English were killed in Hermes Street")—a frantic crowd deserted the shops, the workshops, the offices, and schools and rushed to get out of the old city before the walls closed. Distraught women who had left their children home alone, men with sick wives, young students and frightened old people ran like mad in a desperate attempt to leave in time.

The majority of people always moved to the Hadjisav-vas gate. But often, as the stream of people pushed forward in confusion like a multi-colored, elongated caterpillar with a kind of a head and thousands of little feet all twitching out of rhythm (like an animal in a school play), a voice was often heard announcing:

"The Hadjisavvas gate has been closed!"

The voice passed over the heads undiminished in its power by the cries of despair that arose, affecting those at the back with the same force as those at the front.

"Closed?" some echoed.

"Mother of God, my children!"

The stream stopped for a second (the head of the cat-erpillar paused in thought), and then the entire mass turned as a unit, as if it had been given some subconscious directions, to another gate. And if it found that gate closed (the cries were even more dramatic: "Mother of God, my children!") it rushed breathlessly, without any sign of fatigue or flagging, on to the next. And precisely when the agony reached its peak, the si-rens blared and the megaphones of the police cars announced:

"Curfew! Curfew! Everybody go home at once! The police will open fire!"

Go home? How? The crowd became paralyzed and placid, the cry was now barely audible, frightened, "Holy Vir-gin, my children." The head of the caterpillar thought again for an instant, its thousands of feet quivering in suspension for a second, then it was off in the direction of the nearest gate. If that was now closed, the people would press on in the hopes that after many hours (endless hours), they would be allowed to return home to the children left alone, to the sick wives, to take them the purchases in the bags they were carrying.

At the closed gates, the English enjoyed (I use the word emphatically, they enjoyed) the agony of the crowd. They cursed at the people, they shoved them with the butts of their rifles, kicked them with their boots, separated them into groups with their bayonets, and shot anyone who tried to make an escape across the moat, even women and children. (Why was that woman so impatient, so determined to get home that she tried to run through the moat? What happens now to her children left alone?)

In the relentless summer sun or the chilling winter rain, the crowd waited for hours at the gates. It was revenge and punishment for the incident. A decision suddenly came from somewhere that they could pass, but must be home in half an hour. But how could they get home in half an hour? What other enjoyment did the English plan to get out of them? Thousands of cars (were there so many cars in all of Nicosia?), bicycles, pedestrians, were all packed together in a sweaty mass that squirmed, pushed, and fought hopelessly to find a little space to break free.

A woman begged in a cracked monotone ("Take me with you, my children are alone!").

"Mother of God, a quarter of an hour gone!"

The drama took place outside the walls as well, where another crowd watched and waited. At the sound of the sirens or news of an incident (and it never came swiftly out here), another frantic group, mostly women and children, rushed into the streets ("What has happened?").

If someone from the old city happened by, they fell upon him as a group.

"I don't know, I left before they closed the walls."

"Did you see my husband?" (Twenty, fifty voices together would yell, "Did you see my husband?").

"My son?" (Twenty, fifty voices would yell, "Did you see my son?").

When someone else from the city appeared, they all immediately abandoned the first man to get the latest news. (See how you can throw away something of no use? How you give up on a used-up tale?)

"Did they open the walls yet?"

"No, they say that somebody important was killed."

No one tried to shade the truth to spare the feelings of the women. How could you hide anything, when they would learn it in five minutes anyway? What good would it serve?

(At the beginning of this section I drew a line between the old and new city of Nicosia, although I said they were closely interwoven. No, I'm not sure such a division really exists. Half of our heart beat with the old city, the other half beat with the suburbs, every house seemed to be half within the walls and half outside of them. Nicosia did not jump the walls "free of the memories of the conquerors" (did I really say such a thing?). The new city did not break free from the past; it could not break free from the past; it had been built on the same foundation of history.)

SOMETIMES, most of the people managed to leave before the walls closed. But that only made the English angry, and, on the pretext that all establishments within the walls had to be searched before the occupants could leave, they forced the proprietors to return the next morning (The radio announced, "Anyone who has offices, stores, or workshops within the walls . . . "). And the people would sit in the closed stores or offices for as much as twenty-four hours waiting in vain for a patrol to come and make a search. For the English would never come.

And it was not only the curfews which disrupted life, but also the rumors.

"They hit a jeep on Hippocrates Street."

Instantly the running starts (all that commotion that I just described, and the closing of the offices and shops). And in the midst of this anxiety and agony, one suddenly hears contradictory information ("It's a lie? Yes, not true at all." You doubt for a moment, hesitate. But it really is not true).

So the crowd turns back to their offices and shops with attentive ears, ready to take in the next piece of news.

I must add, however, that this mad, crowded exodus at any report of an incident had a useful purpose; it aided the escape of the patriots. It took a while for the British to realize the fact, but eventually they caught on and did not impose curfews immediately after an incident.

Even worse than the stress of the first hours of a curfew was the terrible quiet that followed. The city was dead, abandoned (what kind of city was this?), with only the noise of boots and jeeps resounding on the streets or knocking against the walls with the bolted doors—a dull sound like an irresponsible pendulum with a confused, erratic swing. (During the curfews the city reminded me of a picture in an English story about the plague epidemic in London. When was that? Where did I read about it? Where?)

Shut up in our house, we rusted from boredom, our minds became warped by worry and nervousness. The English patrolled the streets and walked in the yards, they blackened their faces during the nights so that we would not be able to see them. They climbed on the roofs and terraces and watched us through the windows and skylights (like the Kalikanzari, those mischievous sprites that wreak havoc during the twelve days of Christmas). Little by little they grew to like secret surveillance if they could remain secret, and set up observation points in kiosks, or behind Venetian shudders and Turkish lattices.

The first day of the curfew they gathered the men and boys of fifteen and older in the yard of the school and kept us standing for hours with no water or food—usually they forced us to take off our shoes as well—until it was our turn (and how long it took) to be interrogated or pass before the informer. Covered by a black hood, he would scrutinize us through the two little holes and point out suspects. I will never forget how those eyes appeared to me on one occasion. No, they weren't eyes, they were blades, they were razor-like teeth, they were ice. And there was fear in them, cold fear (I clearly saw the fear in those eyes). The black hood separated the man from the rest of the community, the rest of humanity; it denied him a personality. He now had no head, no voice; he could only communicate with a yellow, shaky, outstretched finger. And the eyes, when he pointed, became even more razor-like, even more frozen.

Later, I often saw in my dreams the eyes of the informer looking through the twin pierced holes. I would observe them become larger and larger, to emerge from behind the hood, and suck me into their enormous whirlpool. Or they would fall at my feet with a supplicating look, or their coldness would come alive and the hood would be covered with snow and the north wind would howl and I would shiver and wrap myself in my blankets.

Those cold, terrifying eyes had complete authority over us. The English placed their final hopes on them. They saw with them, they believed in them rather than in their own eyes. Those eyes ruled the English and us. (Did those hollow, petrified eyes have any useful purpose, I wonder?)

When the interrogations were finished, we returned home exhausted, crushed with hunger and sick with thirst. In those houses where a father or a son did not return, the sound of cries and lamentations erupted from women and children. These desperate voices went unacknowledged and unconsoled, a small private grief in the larger drama of the curfew. (The neighborhood was powerless to offer relief or consolation. What could be said when everyone knew very well what it meant to have that terrible finger pointed at you, knew very well what it meant to be taken to the interrogation rooms of Omorphita and Platres "for a chat"?)

DURING THE FIRST CURFEWS the radio was our constant companion. It brought the cherished "Voice of Athens" to lighten our boredom and solitude ("Our Cypriot Brothers"). I have already described how the radio rose up from the table when Athens came on the air and how we held it tightly to our breast when Athens spoke to us from close by, as if its warm breath caressed us. ("Yes, tell us how we are worthy of Greece.") How different that voice sounded during the curfew —as if it came from another world, as if it had the color of another world.

But the English quickly managed to jam the transmission, and we were left on our own. I remember how we glued an ear to the radio, how we struggled to seize a single word or several broken sporadic syllables that we attempted to join together in comprehensible units. Even if no meaning could be found (why did it have to be comprehensible?), it was sufficient for us to catch a word or to make out a couple of syllables. It was enough for us to know a cherished voice was speaking to us. What did it matter if we could not hear what was said?

Sometimes, however, a bit more, a clause or sentence, managed to come through.

"Father, I heard Athens!" (with the same joy one had for those first bombs, almost exactly the same joy—"Father, I heard Athens!").

THERE WAS a special kind of curfew called the "permanent youth curfew," which effectively imprisoned boys and girls in their homes while their young lives rotted away. Youth disappeared from the streets and with them went the last remnants of life. The nightspots still open were deserted; the movie theaters still showing films were empty. Songs (if there were any) were empty; smiles (if there were any) were empty; love itself seemed empty. The atmosphere of the outside world became now serious and subdued. (Isn't there a story they tell about an evil witch who grew old suddenly? She gave her years and wrinkles to the houses, to the trees ("for you, the wrinkles of my face") and to the people ("for you, the wrinkles of my heart"). The blue skies and the sun searched everywhere for something young, and spring, left alone, lost all sense of purpose.) The streets of the city no longer looked the same. Nicosia was locked up when her young people were locked up.

That was not all. There were the lost wages of a youth, the lost salary of a girl. And there were homes that would go hungry without those wages and salaries.

The first days of the curfew, the imprisoned teenagers pressed against the glass of the windows, behind every window a pair of eyes (just as I had described the younger children in the story of the ball). Little by little as the nerves wore out and patience ended, the eyes thinned out and eventually vanished.

In conjunction with the curfews came the communal fines. Thousands of pounds of fines which were levied after "big incidents." They were apportioned by some unspecified criteria and collected at once without extensions or leniency. Long lists of names filled the newspapers. Those lists were similar to the voices of the town criers of old days who announced the fines and punishments of the Turkish officials during Ottoman times.

The procedure of the fines, as everything else the English did, was monotonously the same. First they called on all of the people in the area of the "incident" to provide information about it. In the villages, they gathered all the men together and coaxed them to start with ("We know the whole village is not to blame; we know it is only a few terrorists"). They explained the reasons why the village should betray the perpetrators ("Why should innocent people be made to pay? Think about your responsibility to your families"). They then passed out pieces of white paper so that the men could secretly and anonymously write what they knew. Inevitably, these pieces of paper came back blank, as white of betrayal as when they were handed out, either unmarked and unfolded, or, if folded, with an ironic message such as a crude drawing of a Greek flag, or "Long Live Greece," or a more simple and direct insult. A heavy communal fine would be announced the next morning, unbearable for such a small village.

Besides the fines and curfews, there were other special punishments for "incidents." A house or store directly connected to an "incident" was demolished and the neighboring buildings evacuated and sealed. With what misery people stood at a distance and looked at their little house for the last time before it was shattered into ruins. What sorrow accompanied the wrenching departure of those forced to evacuate. All of the possessions had been piled hastily beside the street before the prescribed hour when the house would be sealed. Small children cried, and old women howled because they haphazardly, almost subconsciously, would remember a son who had passed away and become stricken with grief again.

And I remember the tragedy of those who had no money to rent a new house, of those who had no money even to pay for their things to be moved. And I remember the neighborhood (that proud neighborhood) finding another house, finding a car, and moving the family.

The doors of the house were closed and nailed shut. A sign was put on the front that announced the evacuation, forbade life in the structure, and effectively declared the house haunted. Sometimes people passing would pause and read the notice. At other times, they would stop and observe the house from a distance for a long time.

IN OUR HOUSE, we had an antidote for the endless days of the curfew, an inexhaustible subject of diversion, always ready at hand, which bound us together, "our" Nikos. During the difficult hours of confinement, the four of us in the house gathered together around Nikos.

"Where is he now, do you think?"

A thousand times the same question ("Where is he now?"). Our thoughts would fly over the mountains and plains in search of him. We considered the areas of recent fighting, we groped into secret hide-outs, we secretly entered the monasteries of Kykko or Machairas late at night, and climbed the rocky peaks of the Pentadactylos.

Our mother would talk more than the rest of us. She would cry more than the rest of us (no, I think she simply produced more tears).

With our absorption in Nikos, our concentration on Nikos, how could the curfews touch us, how could they make their presence felt in our house? How could time weigh upon us, when, with the departure of Nikos, we lived outside of time?

I was tortured by the desire to find a way to write to Nikos (not really to write, but to cry out), to ask his forgiveness for having misunderstood him.

"It is very difficult," said my father.

"Just two little words," I begged, "Stalo" (I said "Stalo" not as a falling anchor, but light, without a punctuation mark).

"I don't know a way, I tell you."

Until one day, though, I threatened her, as a little child threatens.

"Stalo," (with accents this time, accents "grave") "if I don't write to Nikos, I don't know what crazy thing I might do."

It appears that I said exactly what was needed, because she was stunned. She regarded me for a second, several seconds. She did not drag out that old look from the history books this time. She understood that this was a different kind of threat. She was weighing me.

A pause. She turned her face away from me. No, I will not break the silence. You will break it. I have said what I have to say.

And she broke it.

"Write your letter."

I wrote a long letter ("You can't use names." "Absolutely not." "You can't sign your name." "Absolutely not"). Why sign it? Did I need to sign a letter to Nikos? I wrote with a little ink and a lot of tears, as children do.

Stalo refused it.

"One page only."

(A page is not enough, Stalo. "Stalo" this time without accents.) It could not be longer. It would have to be hidden in socks, in shoes, in blouses, in shirtsleeves, in the plaster casts of fake broken arms, in mouths. Did I realize how many people would be uselessly put in danger for my little letter?

"Not uselessly, Stalo."

I filled out one thin page with small, closely packed letters and gave it to her ("OK, now?" "All right"). She folded it and hid it in her bosom.

"Only this one time." (She was almost angry. No, not almost, she was angry.)

"Only this one time, Stalo."

I still feared that she might refuse in the end. I was afraid to say anything further, to press her, to ask when she would send it. She kept talking (I think I divined the reason she kept talking, and became worried).

"You know I would not even do this for mother!" (In our story, I have no name, and even if I had, Stalo would not have mentioned it in any of our conversations. That's how I began with her, and that's how I have continued with her).

"I know, Stalo."

What could she do with me, when I acted so childish?

"It was necessary, Stalo" (a "Stalo" to sweeten her and hold her to her "yes").

She was not certain her friend would "hand it on" (that "hand it on" must have been a phrase of the organization).

I knew there was no friend but did not dare to say so.

"I understand the difficulties, Stalo" (Let's end this at last, Stalo, in the name of God).

And my letter set off warm from my tears and Stalo's bosom. Whatever delays it might endure, it would still arrive full of warmth. And I knew that no matter wherever it went, however it traveled, it would be able to find its own way to Nikos.

WE KEPT IT A SECRET from mother and father. Stalo had stressed this from the beginning.

"Take care, not a word to anyone."

"Are you joking, Stalo?"

The next day she said that she had given the letter to her friend and persuaded her to "pass it on." (Again that same phrase. Why do you keep using phrases that betray you, Stalo, that give you away? Do girls, no matter how well they can hide revolvers in their purses, really fit into secret organizations?)

I did not challenge her about her "friend," as I wanted to stay on her good side until my letter had been sent. But my patience did not last. One day, I retorted.

"Stalo, there is no 'friend.'"

She looked at me with that same inquisitive, militant gaze and did not answer.

She was very angry with me for a few days. Then, suddenly, everything changed. One evening, she took me aside and spoke in a low voice, just a whisper containing the weight only of consonants, not a trace of the light, airy tone of superficial, revealing vowels.

"He sent us his watch to be repaired."

My heart skipped a beat.

"Who? Nikos?"

She did not answer me (Stalo? Nikos, Stalo?).

"No."

A long dreamy, hypnotized "no," as if she wanted to reassure herself that she was doing the right thing, a slow "no" that drifted off into space, like the very first "no" we recorded in our notebooks in school.

"Then who?"

"The old guy."

A sweeter phrase was never uttered in a sweeter way.

The old guy. I seized her in my arms at the words, so that neither she nor the words could escape me.

"Stalo!"

"If you could only have seen how we kissed it, how we pressed it to our lips!"

(Stalo, you finally confided in me. And what a beautiful first exchange you chose, what a fine moment you brought to our home, like the lit candles we strove to bring home from church at Epiphany without extinguishing their tiny flames.)

"The old guy!"

84

FROM THAT DAY ON, Stalo and I conversed regularly; how special these secret intimate exchanges were. No meetings of lovers could ever compare to them. But I never managed to persuade her to get me into the Organization. She continually deflected my requests. And I was desperately awaiting some sign from Nikos.

"Could it be that he didn't get my letter?"

"But he will never write you!" (You are a child! Surely you realize that he can never answer you!)

He will never answer me? How could he not answer that letter? (If you knew what I wrote, Stalo, even you would think that he would answer.) At times I would cast a questioning gaze in her direction, and every now and then I gave halting, tentative voice to my innermost fears and suspicions.

"But you did send it, didn't you, Stalo?"

She became quite short with me.

"I sent it, I told you."

Every so often the English would come to search the house and interrogate us about Nikos. During the night they would creep into the yard barefoot and hide. If we happened to go out for any reason, we would stumble over a soldier and it would scare us half to death.

My mother lived in terror.

"What if Nikos does something crazy and tries to come here during the night? Mother of God, guide him!"

"He can't possibly make a mistake like that, Mother."

"I'm not so sure, he's just a child."

"He is not a child any more, Mother."

But Nikos was still a bit of a child—apparently more than just a bit. One day the man from the electric company (if he really was a man from the electric company) entered the house to read the meter and quietly whispered to mother:

"Your son wants a photograph."

"My son!" (I can't capture that sound).

Deep within her, mother felt a dizziness that tried to overcome her, but, as if it realized its error, it quickly subsided.

"Your son!" The house had taken up the words. (As if it were a fairy tale. "My Queen, I come from your son.") The living room whispered it, his bedroom caressed it, his books pressed it into the pages (just as they had pressed the flowers that he had gathered and inserted into them), the basement echoed in a deep bass, "your son!"

"My son" (it's a wise tongue which can express this in one uninterrupted syllable).

The house answered: Your son.

For some time mother kept the conversation going.

No, the man had not come from her son. Others had sent him.

"But did he know him?"

No, they had never met. (The house did not echo that "no.")

"Did he know where he was?"

No. (The living room, bedroom, books, and basement stayed silent.)

(You say "no" too many times to my mother, friend. Tell her something, tell her a little lie if you have to.)

Mother seemed confused. She glanced around with a distracted look. She lost her sense of balance (how delicate is our sense of balance). But just for a second, she quickly pulled herself together. She remembered that her son wanted a photograph.

"I'll bring one right away, my boy."

And she found one. She held it tightly to her breast. We were all in it, with our arms around one another, laughing and happy, and it had a pink ribbon around the edges.

Mother kissed it and cried.

"Nikos, my son!" ("My son," the house echoed.)

A bit later she asked:

"May I write a note?"

"That was not part of my instructions, I can't take it."

"May I write a few words on the back of the photograph?"

"I don't know."

"I'll make them as though they had been on there for years." ("Two little words, my boy, just two little words.") (Two little words, the house begged.)

She wrote them. She wrote the message of a mother, she added the warm kiss of a mother, the distressed touch of a mother, all of which had to be reduced to two little words, as if it had been written years in the past. (Do mothers have old words and new words? Do mothers need more than two words?)

"He shouldn't worry about us."

86

"And have them tell him," she whispered, "to take care not to come home. Day and night there are soldiers watching."

"And have them tell him . . ."

"And . . ." (there were quite a few more "ands" and some more tears).

What news my mother had for us when we returned home later, what an unexpected, joyous news. Still, I was expecting more.

"Was there no message for me, Mother?"

"What message? There wasn't a message to anyone."

Now a suspicion began to torment me that he had not received my letter.

"You silly boy," Stalo said to me. "How could you ever join the Organization?"

THE STRUGGLE went on fiercely and relentlessly. Only a few homes did not have one of its own among those killed, or hanged, or "wanted," or in prison or in a concentration camp. The whole island was caught up in the effort, was intoxicated with resistance, flushed like a child's cheeks during a crazy, reckless game. It still amazes me how death seemed to lose its meaning for them. They mocked it, they dared it, as if common sense no longer functioned. They felt that they were living by default.

In addition to the armed rebellion, the Passive Resistance began to upset the workings of the English administrative machine. A boycott was instituted against all goods imported from England; English products disappeared from the shelves of stores and cupboards of private homes. There were mass demonstrations. These actions gave the general population a chance to have a share in the struggle for independence, to be involved on a daily basis. During the boycott, for example, many families refused to buy cloth manufactured in England and sought out material made by traditional Cypriot methods. In the villages, the old looms reappeared and even the girls in the city began wearing cloth made from these looms—called "alajia." (How pretty they looked in their garments of alajia.) Even children of four and five years old made their contribution to the boycott.

"Nothing English, Mother!" (spoken in that stubborn Cypriot voice that warned and threatened).

ONE ASPECT of the non-violent protests was the contest over the flag. (Is it still necessary to say "Greek" flag?) It would be planted on inaccessible peaks of mountains, on the tops of trees, on lampposts, on rooftops—the light blue of the flag merging with the light blue of the sky (How they complemented each other!).

The English climbed everywhere to take them down (how eager they were for the task), but this was not as easy as one would think, since the shafts of the lampposts and the trunks of the trees had been well greased with fat. It added another comic element to the rebellion, but later the game became deadly when some soldiers were killed by bombs fastened to the flagpoles. After that, the English no longer dared and would force us to do it.

The flags were not limited to trees and lampposts. They were everywhere, especially on the roofs of schools. Every morning there was a Greek flag merrily greeting the children as they arrived at school.

The children always cheered at the sight of it. The little voices became entangled in the flapping of the flag, bounced off the roof tiles, echoed off the water pipes, and returned to the schoolyard even louder, until an English patrol arrived to take down the flag.

The problem confronting the English was more difficult at the schools than on the streets. The teachers refused point blank to go up on the roof and take down the flag. (What? Take the Greek flag down right before the eyes of their students?) The pupils also refused. (What? Take a Greek flag down with their teachers watching?)

At the elementary school in our neighborhood there was an "incident" that is worth mentioning. The soldiers had taken a small boy in the fifth grade and were trying to force him to climb up and remove a flag improvised (improvised? watch your language) from poorly dyed cloth (so poorly dyed, in fact, that the blue was not recognizable as blue).

Yiorgakis was the liveliest boy at school, and there was no one whom he wouldn't tease. He was the admired leader of the neighborhood kids.

"Yiorgakis!" ("Yiorgakis!" The chant went up from the schoolyard, the corridors, and the classrooms.)

He looked (really a quick glance, half a second, full of hate) at the gun of the English man who was prodding him in the back. Another glance back ("What exactly are you?" his look seemed to ask).

Then he saw the entire school hanging upon his movements ("What was all this commotion so early in the morning?").

Then a silence. Yiorgakis realized that his great moment had arrived. He was only eleven years old, but the moment was already there waiting for him, he was sure that an unavoidable and unyielding moment had arrived.

He looked again at his schoolmates, lifted his head just a little (no, not a little, to the heavens) as if pondering his fate. He turned his eyes to look up to the flag for one second, then two, three. How beautiful it seemed (yet it was, as I said, very badly dyed). He weighed it. (How much does a flag weigh? How heavy is a Greek flag?) He talked to it absent-mindedly. Then he lowered his head and walked slowly, just like a condemned prisoner who had said his last prayer and was ready to meet his end (All right. Let's go).

(Let's go? But where are we going? Your friends are holding their breath, Yiorgakis. The entire school is holding its breath. What did the flag say to you, Yiorgakis? Did it give its consent?)

The Englishman was encouraged by Yiorgakis's demeanor and gave him another hard push.

"Come on!"

The boy started forward again. He went only a few steps (*"Good boy!"*), but then suddenly bent down. He made a sudden twist and was off running.

Behind him enthusiastic cheers and shouts went up. The school building itself was throwing its tiles in the air.

The furious soldier began to hunt him down. His voice was harsh and angry.

"Stop! I'll shoot you! Stop! I'll shoot you!"

The teachers grew frightened. (Here is one moment where we children are different. Remember that we talked about this before.) Just as Yiorgakis completed his first circuit of the school, they tried to end his great moment.

"Stop now! He will kill you!"

(The teachers, not the students—students do not withdraw their support so quickly, do not abandon great moments so easily. They were already running beside Yiorgakis. They ran in front of him, some behind him, to protect him.)

90

Yiorgakis never looked back.

"*I'll shoot you, I said!*"

I don't know what the other Englishmen might have remembered of their history lessons, but they did not get involved. They only watched, as if they were looking down from the walls of Troy into the moat (did Troy have a moat?). Maybe they did not want to embarrass their friend. ("Of course you don't need any help with this little boy.")

The boy with the Englishman behind him passed a second time, then a third. Each time the enthusiastic cheers and cries became louder and louder. On the fourth, Yiorgakis fell down exhausted (he really was a little boy). The Englishman did not give him time to catch his breath. He grabbed him immediately by the collar.

"*Come on!*"

Come on? One second, two seconds, one century, two centuries, of fearful anticipation. And all of sudden Yiorgakis's little voice was heard, but deeper and more authoritative than ever before.

"*No!*" (Perhaps it was the only English word he knew.)

The eucalyptus trees quivered, the pages of the history books on the desks fluttered open, the spigots in school shot water into the air.

The Englishman angrily pulled Yiorgakis up and tried to make him stand.

"*Come on, I said!*"

Yiorgakis fell back to ground.

"*No!*" (Again the eucalyptus trees quivered, the water shot from the spigots. The pages flew out of the history books and surrounded the flag fluttering over the scene.)

The nerves of the Englishman could stand no more. He stuck his nose into the little boy's face.

"*I'll kill you, bastard!*"

Yes, the man would surely kill him now. Yiorgakis could see it, and he got to his feet. (Got up? Is that the right description? He took a full five minutes for one leg, and a full five minutes for the other.)

"Let's go."

Everyone followed the scene in silence. They were afraid that it had come to an end. (The Trojans now leaned over the walls.) Yiorgakis looked all around him for another five minutes and saw them—not looked at them, but saw them

91

—saw the school inspired by his great moment, petrified in his great moment, saw his classmates. (But what had happened? They were no longer cheering; where had they withdrawn, why weren't they still at their posts?) He saw his teachers (but something else happened with them as well; they were not yelling "stop" any more). He instinctively understood that this was one of those defining moments when outside intervention cannot help you, cannot even affect you, when encouragement and cheers would have no impact. He looked again at the flag, and had to shake his head at the joke. Why was this poorly made flag, in which the blue was not even blue, linked by fate to his destiny? If only he knew who had been responsible for that flag. He'd find out who was responsible for it.

Again he advanced one step, then a second step, but balked at a third. With a lightning quick motion, he turned and tripped the Englishman, put him flat on his back on the ground (What a trip that was, put it next to the stones of the village boys from Mesaoria). Yiorgakis was halfway across the field to jump the fence when the stunned Englishman grabbed his gun from the mud and took aim, but at that moment history intervened (was it history intervening?). Just as Ibrahim Pasha searched the battlefield of Maniaki to find the body of Papaflessas and pay tribute to a "real man," so the English sergeant honored the bravery of an eleven-year-old boy.

"*No! Stop it!*"

The next second Yiorgakis jumped the fence and was gone. And running after him, trying to catch up, came the cheers of the children and the pages of history.

SEVERAL TIMES I have referred to the comic aspects of the rebellion without making any real attempt to explain or analyze them. Could it be that they all arose from the inherent drama of the situation, that they were not really comic. Perhaps, at bottom, there was absolutely nothing comic about them. I'm not sure. If I were writing a play, I would probably be inclined to create in a vague, surrealistic style, with no known place or time either (contemporary or historical) without confining myself to the human world situated between laughter and pain. My play would have no beginning or end; it would be fashioned with the backdrop of a smiling blue sky from which comes rain, a cloudy sky that smiled, where the heavens play with clods of earth, and where a child plays with the stars. All of this would be artificial but it would also be real, like the little donkey—a very real little donkey—that walked up and down in downtown Nicosia one day bearing a sign on its back.

"My Field-Marshal, I surrender!"

This was the comic response to the ludicrous proposal of the governor that all the "terrorists" should turn themselves in.

The little donkey was well-cast for his part, looking to the right, then to the left, with its long tail making sweeping half-circles behind it. Then the donkey went over to the shop windows, observing the displays, interpreting the scenes, adding discoveries to our timeless surrealistic drama.

I began by saying that I was not sure where the comic elements came from, but we all took refuge in them, cherished the needed relief they provided from the terrible, intense strain of the times.

93

THE STRUGGLE reached the heavens (in fact took them by storm) when, in March, Gregoris Afxentiou, already wounded, held off an entire English regiment for ten hours. The soldiers were puzzled and embarrassed. They were not prepared for Thermopylae (if in fact this was simply a Thermopylae). No one had told them how to handle a Thermopylae. In their desperation, they burnt Gregoris alive in his refuge. And when they set fire to him, they also set fire to their schoolbook stories, their first contact with history in the forgotten refuge of their childhood years.

The British commander simply said:

"It was a jolly good show!"

Show? The same mangled vocabulary again? Yes, the same (the same as that used by the "winner" at Thermopylae). But who cared about their mangled vocabulary? The leaflets would appear, the leaflets would provide the proper words, would make of Gregoris a poem, a song.

> The echo did not repeat
> The words were too heavy to be carried by the wind . . .
>
> How did you sign, Gregoris?
> With flashes of lightning?
> With what shouts of battle,
> With what words did you choose to wrap yourself in?
> What thunder bolt did you embrace
> And enmeshed together fall earthward?
> And the earth did not believe your hand touched it,
> And the earth shuddered that your forehead touched it,
> And the soil groped for your hand,
> And the earth reached out to caress your hair.
> What field did you plough up in your game,
> What canyons did you make in the sky when you kicked at it?
> What joke was this, Gregoris?
> What did you put into our pockets which made us sink?
> Now how will we cope, how will we carry on,
> With what drill of blood will we water the legacy you gave us?

Later an English voice would come from afar, in a song from London:

Come out, come out, young Gregory,
There's guns all round your cave.
The sun's rising over the mountains
And you've only one life to save.

. . . .

You bleed, you bleed, young Gregory,
Now come out without shame.
A wounded man may save his life
And there'll be none to blame.

But still young Gregory's shooting
And the soldiers have no rest
And the hours pass in darkness
And the sun goes to the west.

Machine-guns go to fetch him,
Grenades are next to try,
Tear-gas is sent to blind him,
The man who will not die.

Then the petrol barrels lumber
Out of soldiers' sight,
And the bullets set them burning
And the cave is blazing bright.

. . . .

And dynamite and petrol
Are piled among the rocks,
For when the hounds are wearied
All's fair to kill a fox.

. . . .

Then the Governor came to tell them
How bravely they had done,
For the regiment gained new honour
When sixty men killed one.

But when brother speaks to brother
And father speaks to son,
In the memory of his people
Young Gregory lives on.

Father read this ballad to us, and translated it with emotion, with such emotion that we were afraid his feelings for the old "Ally" were reviving, that he was experiencing again that feeling which had caused tears during the trial of the crew of the *Saint George* (you recall—when father, mother, and all Greeks were like children).

IN APRIL, the bad news finally came to our home. It hit like a cyclone and ripped our house from its foundation and left it smashed on the ground wrapped up in a Greek flag.

I still vividly recall that terrible night. I still recall how that ill-omened night had the hooked claws of a vulture, the eyes of an owl.

We had just gone to bed when hard knocks crashed against the door. Although we were accustomed to this pounding, it always scared us. I don't know why, but that night we were more frightened than usual.

"Mother of God" (always "Mother of God"), "my son!" my mother said. (Why did she add those last words on that night? What kind of premonition did she have, how long had it been gnawing at her without her letting it show?) ("Mother of God!" we all echoed silently.)

Father went to open the door and we trailed behind him.

There were two Englishmen and a Turkish constable.

"Is this the house of Nikos Drakos?"

"Yes, I'm his father."

"*He is killed.*"

Killed? (No, not this word, for the love of God, not this knife to the heart, not this darkness, this abyss. Can someone else narrate this for me?)

No, let's turn our backs and skip this scene. Don't look at mother, don't look at father, turn away from us all. Don't say anything further. Don't go on. Let that phrase stand alone (like the eyes of the traitor under his hood). Leave us alone to bear the burden.

At some point (was it right away, an hour later, or a thousand years later?) they told father that they had the body at the Pendayia Hospital and he would have to go and identify it.

Father, apparently, was still able to take in what was going on around him, since he turned to look at us. Thick, silent tears ran down his cheeks. (How can I avoid the usual clichés about grief?) As he came toward us, he thought for a second as if, dazed, he had forgotten what to do. Then he embraced us, as if to make sure that he still existed. He embraced mother, then Stalo, and finally me. After the embraces, he tried to speak (perhaps to say "courage" or some such thing) but couldn't manage it. The sobs that he had kept back suddenly broke free and choked his words.

They took him and left.

They had said "only the father." Were we to stay behind? I rushed out into the street half-naked, like a madman, to find a car. And we arrived at Pendayia Hospital, thirty miles away, almost exactly at the same time as the jeep that took father.

The guard stopped us at the gate.

"We are the family of the person who was killed," Stalo said.

The guard took a look in the car, saw it was loaded with tears, loaded with grief, and let us pass.

"All right."

It seemed that father expected us because when we suddenly came upon him in the corridor of the hospital he was not surprised at all and did not even ask why we were there. After a while, they called his name, and he went up. He was calm now, erect, standing tall, a match for this great moment, a match for his son.

We all followed behind him as we followed behind him on the nights when the English soldiers came to the house and beat on the door. No one tried to stop us. Perhaps they realized that nothing in the world would have been able to do it. (Close your eyes and try to imagine that silent, tense, endless walk of twenty steps down the corridor of the hospital. I cannot help you with that.)

On a bed lay our Nikos. He wore the uniform of a guerrilla. His face was bloody, his glassy eyes were wide-open as if they were expecting us. Father stood before the body with his hat in his hand and his eyes fixed on that dear face.

"He's your son?"

"Yes."

(This "yes" was not meant to be received only by human beings, someone beyond the human audience was asking.)

There was a brief interval during which father stood motionless and withdrawn, looking down at Nikos. The rest of us were a few steps behind him. He must have been saying something to his dead son, he would have had something to say. He bent down to close the eyes, perhaps so they would not have to see the tears of the mother and children that were about to burst forth (mothers and children cry a lot), that he felt swelling up behind him, threatening to destroy the self-restraint he had put on for "great moments." But he wasn't quick enough, mother intervened.

"Don't close them!"

It was a fierce, desperate cry. And, following her lead, we all, including father now, overturned the "great moment" and fell upon the body of Nikos in one confused mass. We kissed him, caressed the hair, and spoke to him, all at once, each one imparting his own private message (I asked, over and over again, if he had gotten my letter).

Father's voice went up an octave, so that it sounded like a child's; he was weeping now like a child.

After a while they managed to get us to leave. (Time became rather vague again. Someone else will have to calculate it somehow, so the gaps disappear from the narrative.) We spent the night outside in front of the hospital, huddled together, one mass of tears.

We waited in vain. In vain we expected to caress him again. In the morning they would not let us have the body for burial.

They (what were they thinking?) would bury him in the grounds of the Central Prison, they told us.

What? They would not give us our Nikos, her son, his son? They would not give the parents their son?

Skip this scene. Leave mother alone to yell like a madwoman, leave her alone to tear out her hair. Leave father alone, too.

When we returned to the house we were no longer people, but shades, shells of our former selves. What kind of home was waiting for us now? (No, it was not waiting for us, it was waiting for Nikos, and we did not bring him. The house was waiting for Nikos and we did not even bring his body.)

As soon as we arrived, men, women, and children hurried over to lend us support, to remind us of the cause and "great moments." We were oblivious to them.

THE NEWSPAPERS were filled with descriptions of the battle. They printed large photographs of Nikos (old, tender pictures with the cap, the eager eyes, and the smile of high school). They related how the young squad leader had stayed behind to cover the escape of his men.

Stop a second. Squad leader? Nikos was a squad leader? I suddenly switched into a fantasy world. Great moments found me an easy target now and they took over my mind (children are always easy targets for great moments). These fantasies said that I would be appointed as the bridgehead for our grieving home so that gradually the great moments would return to the others too. They were obviously in error. What others, and why gradually? Mother already had covered Nikos's bed with a Greek flag. (His small room, facing the garden, was turned into our little chapel.)

It was one thing that mother fussed with the room and the Greek flag (what did you expect of a mother?). (It was not, I should add, exactly a real flag. She had fashioned it herself with a tear and a stitch, a sob and a stitch, and altered it somehow.) But her grief at not being able to visit Nikos's grave was something else altogether. She begged us to help her.

"They won't allow it, Mother. You know that."

They won't allow it? One morning when we woke up she was gone. We knew instantly where to look for her and ran like mad—father in front, Stalo and I behind—the entire three miles to the prison. There she was, at the entrance, sitting on a rock with a large, thick bouquet of flowers in her arms. It was mother, all right, but it wasn't her either.

"Take her home!" said the guard.

We were afraid that she had lost her mind, like the mother of one of the boys who had been hanged, just twenty years old. That woman had no other family except her son and never accepted that she had lost him. So, for a long time after his death she continued to go to the prison each day with a casserole of food (Remember that solemn hymn, that lonely, frail, weak, sweet voice?).

"For Iakovos my son," she would tell the guards.

And the guards, as they got to know her, took pity on her and took the food.

"For James? OK."

Mother could not be allowed to meet this woman. Instead, we took her to meet the mother of Panayides (I have to

100

give the name) from Yerolakkos. She was a striking old woman, tall and unsmiling. She did not let out a single tear at the hanging of her son. She had loosened her scarf so that her face was visible from the bottom of her chin to the top of her forehead, in defiance against those who dared to touch her son, against the earth, against the sun, against life and death.

"I accept no condolences! I am celebrating!"

When she took you by the hand, she squeezed hard as if to reject your kind intentions, as if to offer her own alternative to your kind intentions. (Not like this, but like this!)

(Yes, but why did she squeeze your hand so hard? What was she after? Was she trying to bolster her own resolve?)

Later, when she caught her son's wife furtively embracing her four children or weeping over them in private, she would yell, "You'll spoil my children! (Why "my" children?) You fool, we dreamed of such glory as this for our house!"

(We can admire such resolve. But why, strange narrator, do these "great moments" cause you the same tears as your own "small moments" at the hospital? Do you find them so similar? You will confuse us and ruin the story.)

AFTER Nikos's death I started to press Stalo again to help me to join the Organization, but each time she found a different excuse to put me off (she sent word but received no answer; perhaps they wanted me to work with school groups; a thousand different excuses). And I had to be patient, to sweeten the sound of my "Stalo," make it even more imploring, caressing, tripping, without a trace of punctuation.

One time, however, a curious "perhaps" escaped from her lips (didn't I tell you that girls aren't really fit for secret organizations?). Perhaps, she said, they did not wish to take us all.

"All? All of whom, Stalo? Stalo, What are you trying to tell me?"

IT DID NOT take me long to realize what she meant. Because Nikos's death was not the only tragedy to strike our home. (How could it be the only one? Fate usually does not have the time to return to the same subject or to come back to the same home. It finishes everything completely in a place before moving on.) In August, heavy knocks struck the door once again, just as before. I say "as before," but it was only "as before" for the English soldiers. There was no "as before" for us. What could be the same with Nikos dead? Nevertheless, the door was still there, and they pounded upon it. And we discovered our error. There was still a margin for terror, there was still a margin for misfortune.

Tragedy knocked at our door again. And we opened it. Father opened it, as he always had (but without his military look and his commanding voice: "I'll answer it"). We did not get up to follow him, we had stopped doing that. How could we know that this time we should have observed the absence of usual practice, that this time we should have ignored his military look and commanding voice? This time they had come for father. (Father, how could we have left you alone?)

He came back with two Englishmen. He looked at us for a second. (Paint that look, find some way to preserve it. Perhaps it will never be repeated.) We leapt to our feet.

"Father!"

And we all rushed to him.

He tried to say something (just as on the night when they had told us about Nikos) but he couldn't manage it. His fingers grasped for us, fumbled for us as if he were blind. (Who used this expression before? May I repeat it?)

They took him and left. The door closed again. It closed for the second time.

SIX DAYS of anguish followed. I'll pass by this anguish without description. Leave us alone to run with our hearts in our throats (just like the wife of Antonis the milkman) from one police station to the next, from one interrogation center to the next, empty, drained, ghost-like.

"No, he is not here." ("No, he is not here." "No he is not here.")

Finally, on the seventh day, we were informed that he was now at the Kokkinotrimithia Detention Camp (we will not comment again on that "Now").

In the detention camp? Father, how can we get along without you? Father, with whom will we talk about Nikos? With whom will you talk about Nikos? How can we remember him if we're not together? How can we share his photographs? What is happening, Father?

You begin to look around you. You enter Nikos's room and look around. You enter father's office and look around. You take it in as though you had never entered it before. Only three of us remain now, you say (did you say it?). We are left without a captain in a fearful tempest.

Without a captain? I lay awake pondering this. Although I was just a child, hurt that I had not been included, that no one had confided in me, I was seized by a joy (yes, joy—don't be afraid I've told you the thoughts that lie within children) that I now would take up the management of our home, given mother's misery.

What thoughts I had! But someone had secretly transformed mother overnight. This strange mother was now saying in front of Nikos's grave and father's barbed wire:

"There are thousands like us!"

Mother, what did you say? You don't really believe that, Mother. You are only doing it to shatter my dreams, to take away my last hope.

OUR HOUSE was experiencing difficult times because, to compound the other blows, we had financial problems. We received a small allowance from the Organization, but it was hardly sufficient. We started selling everything. And whenever the curfews were announced, we never seemed to have enough food on hand.

Every Sunday we went to see father (with all of the preparations I described earlier, the cakes, the buses, the solemn festival outside the detention camp, the eyes nailed to the door that would open, the ears attentive to the creaking of the hinges, creaking that did not offer the promise of an embrace. Only the eyes could embrace through the wire, only those eyes sorrowfully fixed upon a cherished face).

"What was that, Father?"

He tried to give us courage. That heavy pounding upon the door, he says, was History knocking—how did he come up with this idea, in what loneliness had he contemplated this rhetoric and forced me to include it in the story?—History was shaking our house. Is that inconsequential? Is it of no consequence, that History was shaking our house and not our neighbor's?

We would not answer. When we were near him we would allow ourselves private moments. And our private thoughts could not understand the things he said. (Father, let us have a break for a while from "great moments" and History, let us relax. Tonight when we go back to them (in Nikos's room with the Greek flag), and we'll be proud and alert, then we'll answer you.)

Of course, we never mentioned our economic problems to him.

THE NEW SPRING found us honored, but miserable. (The chapters have become smaller as the misfortunes fall quickly, one after another, and ruin and betray your plan for the book.) The Struggle rang the bells, it howled in the trees, it closed doors, it scaled the north winds, it kicked over the ravines (the anonymous fighter in the narrow lanes of Nicosia, Liopetri, Kyriakos Matsis's famous cry "I won't come out alive"). And again the echoing wind was unable to carry his words, and dropped them onto the peaks of the Pentadactylos. And again the English would demolish the stories of their youth and their first contact with history. The melancholy song went:

> Spread the mist
> Don't let the joy of skylarks
> Fall upon the stalks.

A strange story about Liopetri had circulated (in a manner like the illegal pamphlets—where did that idea come from?).

The Irishman Killed in Cyprus

The soldier who died of his injuries following Tuesday's gun battle at Liopetri was Rifleman Daniel Donald Kinsella, aged 20, a regular Soldier of Crumlin, Dublin.

It was a great shock to hear you were killed, Daniel, and that we were the ones who had killed you. We weren't aware that you were fighting against us, we couldn't imagine that you were our enemy. You will tell us, undoubtedly, that great poverty exists in Dublin, that your married women, so very religious, have as many children as they are able to bear—ten, fifteen, even twenty. All of these children flood the streets to find a crust of bread. You will say that your young girls line up on O'Connell Street every afternoon and, with an incredible naïveté, wait for someone to offer them a cup of tea or a ticket to the movies with no strings attached. You will tell us how jobs are scarce and the pay so meager that becoming an English soldier is a viable option, a real solution.

We know all these things. To start with, we know Dublin well. We loved St. Stephen's Green, where in sum-

106

mer's slight, brief rays, a crowd of thousands fills the rows of benches or sits on the grass to bathe in the caress of your pale, anemic sun. St. Stephen's Green is very beautiful, Daniel. Phoenix Park? No, I think it is too large for one to really care for. And then, of course, the Christmas card appearance of Grafton Street and the melancholy, muddy River Liffey (why is it always so mournful?). Doesn't it seem that the Liffey tries to pass by without anyone noticing—it gives the impression of a frightened dog with a skulking head and a tail between its legs, or a hooded traveler on a long journey who has no time to spare a thought, no time to spare a glance along the way? (I heard that the Liffey does not flow through any deceitful tunnels or the moats of old fortifications, and that, as far as anyone knew, it had never done so, that it is a river without memories.) (Yes, can I ask you, Daniel, the falls at Metal Bridge, as they are called, where you used to go every afternoon with your friends when you were a student, are they part of the Liffey?)

I have to admit that I have never visited your suburb of Crumlin, although I was living nearby, but I certainly will go as soon as I visit Ireland again. Is it as beautiful as Templeogue? It has the same houses, the same green? Seriously, what fairy painted your land with such greenness? Who had such a mania for the color in all its various hues and shades? And then, Dun Laoghaire (the way you say it is so strange that I must write it phonetically, "Dan Liry") and the dreaminess of Bray, Howth, and Killiney.

We had read about Killiney, we had lived in the myths and legends of the dense forest before we had ever seen it. Did you know that Killiney has a lot in common with Kyrenia, Daniel? Yes, Kyrenia! A friend of mine has discovered a stand of eucalyptus trees in Killiney, you know. They may be the only eucalyptus trees in Ireland. He took me to see them before he showed me anything else, as if I too had not seen eucalyptus trees for years, as if I too were nostalgic for the hanging hopes, the bent dreams, the broken wings of these strange trees that despite their gloom, despite their drooping earthward, confound the painters by fitting harmoniously into our blue background of sky. The eucalyptus trees in Ireland were exactly the same as the ones at home. They smelled so sweetly in that thin, spidery rain, a unique smell (you know that your own trees don't smell, that your flowers don't smell either). The person who planted them must have truly loved and deeply missed Cyprus.

I can tell you more, Daniel. I know the afternoon placid stillness of your lakes nestled in the hills, they surely are not part of this world. The surfaces of the lakes rise up with excitement for an instant to observe the foreign visitors (even from Cyprus, imagine that), but just for that instant, if you can capture that moment, and then they sink back to the deep, leaving on the top a dead, cold expanse for the reveries of poets.

We have gotten sidetracked and babbled on about other things, Daniel. All we wanted to tell you was that we know these places well, the places that you loved and could never forget. We have loved these places also. We even loved, strange as it may seem, your rain, that never seems to stop even in the middle of summer. We also wanted to say that we know your lifestyle well. We wanted to remind you of the smiles of the Irish girls as they cross the street like swallows. You know that such smiles cannot be found anywhere else in the world. Remember how your girls greet friends and strangers alike with that easy, angelic smile caressing one like love, like the sun, like the rustling of pine trees (I can't find the right simile) and then passes on? (You know this, Daniel, but for all those who don't know, it is necessary to set it down in parentheses.) (In parentheses? No. Everything else can go into parentheses, but those smiles must stay outside of them.) How innocent those smiles are, nothing more than a greeting, a greeting for all, like a ray of the sun.

We have left the subject again, Daniel, but perhaps we had to talk about all these things before coming to the slogans written on your bridges about the struggle in Cyprus (just like the slogans we write on our bridges and houses in Nicosia), and to your newspapers that were captivated by the tale of the heroic little island, and to your poets who sang and cried over the boys on the gallows.

Daniel, you remember the statues in St. Stephen's Green Park? You remember the statue of Major Constance Markievicz? *"A valiant woman who fought for Ireland."* You remember her smile?

In your national museum we wept over the last letters of Francis X. Flood. You know of him, surely. The English shot him at the first signs of spring, on March 14, 1921. He was your age, twenty. No? We will remind you of his letters, we copied them through many tears:

> "My dear Mother,
> I send you a lock of my hair and a statuette of the Virgin Mary that Sister Monica gave me. Pray before it and I shall join my prayers with yours from heaven."

> "My dear father,
> I write to ask you to forgive me for all the worries I have caused you. I feel happy that I depart from life for I am certain that I shall see God. Do not cry and do not wish that I could come back. Think only that I shall wait for you in heaven."

You must also have heard about Sean MacDiarmada. You have his last letter as well, written just a few hours before his execution (they shot Sean in spring, in the month of May).

> "My dear Daly,
> Just two words to say goodbye. I expect in a few hours to join Tom and the others in a better world. I will be shot in the morning. I have nothing to say about this, except that I look on it as part of the day's work. We die that the Irish nation can live. Our blood will rebaptize the motherland. I trust that it is unnecessary to tell you how happy I feel. I am completely sure, as I have always been, that our Ireland can never die."

In the month of May they also shot the poet Thomas MacDonagh. There are some of his mementos in your museum. His collection *Golden Joy* is open to the page of the song "The Coming of Spring":

> The night drips sorrow still
> But tomorrow, dawn will be golden.

There are also the sketches and letters of others, who were shot on May 8, 1916 (What is this mania with May!).

Well, we have the same kind of letters, Daniel. They were written by boys who were twenty (like Francis and yourself), twenty-two, even seventeen. The English did not shoot ours, they hanged them. And, you know, they sang the "Hymn

109

to Liberty" as the ropes tightened around their necks, to the very last second as long as their vocal chords were only able to emit a choked, brief unrecognizable sound. They commenced the hangings in Cyprus in May, just as it happened in your country. I don't know why.

As I'm telling you all these things, I live your struggle just as intensely as I live ours. It is impossible for me not to whisper your first revolutionary proclamation. I read it the same number of times as I had read our first revolutionary leaflet, so much so that at times they would become mixed up and confused in my mind and seem to be a single text (or, at least, we on one side of the paper, and you on the other).

"In the name of God and of the dead generations from which she receives her old tradition of nationhood, Ireland, through us, summons her children to her flag and strives for her freedom. . . .

We declare the right of the people of Ireland to the ownership of Ireland, and to the unfettered control of Irish destinies, to be sovereign and indefensible. . . .

We place the cause of the Irish Republic under the protection of the most High God Whose blessings we invoke upon our arms and we pray that no one who serves that cause will dishonour it by cowardice, inhumanity or rapine. In this supreme hour the Irish Nation must live by its valour and discipline and by the readiness of its children to sacrifice themselves for the common good, prove worthy of the august destiny to which it is called."

And finally, I can't help telling you something else, Daniel. Once I went to your theater (the Abbey, you know it) with a friend from Cyprus. The orchestra (it is strange, but true) did not play the numbers listed in the program at the intermission, but Greek folk songs—Greek folk songs, Daniel. Perhaps they knew my friend and wanted to please him. That's not important. What is important is that the Dance of Zalongo echoed suddenly and unexpectedly in my soul in that far away foreign theater.

And now tell us, Daniel, however many extenuating circumstances you invoke, how could you have come to kill us? I am not sure, of course, if you killed any of the four boys in the silo (if you had only known what those boys were like!). I don't know if you were among the soldiers who set the fire that burned them alive (burning to death the young teacher who had spoken so beautifully to his students about Ireland).

And tell us how it came to pass that we have killed you? Why did you make us do it? We must write to your mother so she knows, we must write to Ireland so it knows, Daniel. When I return to Ireland, I will go without fail to Crumlin to say it; I will knock on the door of your house to say it.

WE HAD a great victory recently—the release of the archbishop. With what rapture we celebrated his return, despite all of our grief and pain. His release gave us a delicious respite of joy. The mournful bells of his exile were now triumphantly reversed. Once more the small children huddled at the feet of their mothers to ask what was happening, and grandmothers spun the golden thread on their spinning wheel, pondering and planning the continuation of the legend that would now be woven ("Once during the night a strange ship anchored off a far away island. Its sails were not sails, its sailors were not sailors. High up on the main masthead . . . And the ship took him and left").

Then came a second victory, the replacement of the governor. We had promised him this defeat, you remember. We had promised it to those pursed, distrustful lips, to that fist, to his "red caps" and commandos (have I been carried away by rhetoric?). We had vowed it on the night he hanged Michael and Andreas.

The old women spread their black mantles on the ground.

"A curse upon you!"

I DON'T KNOW if I have set everything in the right chrono-
logical order. In any case, I would not want to change the sequence of events from the one they have arranged on their own
(there is a reason the narrative has arranged itself in this way; it
has a meaning).

And the problem is not simply with the sequence. I
must also have left many things out of my account. And unfortunately I cannot promise to fill these lacunae.

Sometime earlier (was it before the story of Daniel?) I
should have begun to talk about the Turks. The English, in
their embarrassment and confusion, had incited Turkish mobs
to burn, pillage, and kill. Many nights we saw from our house
the flames burning in Nicosia like large burning cypress trees.
As soon as darkness fell the Turks stirred from the depths of
Asia, from the depths of centuries past, armed with knives and
axes. They poured into streets empty because of the curfews
(they were not bound by the curfew). Their flag bearers went
stripped to the waist and their chests were smeared with the
blood of an ox. So began a story, where and when it would end
no one could tell, for which no one knew who would pay the
price. (Who in Greece would pay the price for this? Who in
Turkey, or in England, or in the rest of the world? Those responsible must be found and brought to account, I tell you.
They must be called to account because we lived for hundreds
of years with these people. But the Turks we saw now were
not the ones we had known earlier. Who had changed them?
Who had collected that rabble? Were they aware of the kind
of fire they were playing with?)

For a long time the Organization counseled self-
restraint and patience ("Don't let the English win the game of
divide and rule"). In the end, that strategy proved impossible
and a civil war blazed. At night, we waited for them and they
waited for us. We organized neighborhood defense groups and
set up all-night sentries and observation posts. We became
hard and merciless. We hid pickaxes and bottle of hydrochloric
acid in our homes. We trained ourselves in self-defense from
sudden attacks and learned how to strike with a knife.

Every day our side had deaths, and so did theirs: men,
women, and children. When you left your house in the morning you weren't sure if you would return alive. You could not
tell on the street if a person was a Greek or a Turk, you did not
know if someone put his hand into his pocket to take out a

113

handkerchief or a pistol. With what searching glances, what suspicions, what constant surveillance did you peer at everyone. From a distance you tried to predict nationality, to interpret intentions. Every bicycle which drew near was suspect; at the passing of each automobile you had an involuntary reaction to protect yourself, and, if it reduced its speed, you threw yourself on the ground. It was a terrible period of bruising conflict on two fronts, with the English and Turks, that continued all day and all night. Nicosia tottered in a daze. Pedestrians were no longer pedestrians. Its street signs no longer provided directions. It was only a surface. It seemed as if someone had taken a knife and scraped the city hollow, leaving just the empty shell. (Do not even use the city's name. It did not even know itself.)

THE NEW GOVERNOR came full of promises. He kept repeating, over and over again, that he was not a "military man" like the previous one, he would go into small chapels to light a candle for "God's help in finding a solution." (This was new.) He recited verses from Shakespeare and flattered the Organization. It was no longer the ignorant and inflexible English propaganda of the past; it was now the experienced, masterful English diplomacy (Why can't they manage to somehow combine the two?).

And one day the Agreement was signed (others can relate the intervening events). After the signing, the lights of the main square blazed, the bells rang, the prisons and concentration camps were emptied, the guerillas came down from the mountains. (Who will describe their parade? The girls showered them with jasmine and the little children ran up to touch them. It was a real parade, not like the ones on the 25th of March or the 28th of October.) And the "wanted" dashed (that is the right word) back to their homes.

Mothers and fathers embraced them and cried. Wives, fiancées, sisters embraced them and cried. Everyone embraced them and cried. (Paint all of Nicosia in one embrace, clinging tightly and crying; render the walls of the city in an embrace. And paint the city throwing its school cap into the air, paint it standing on one leg. Call out its name a thousand times. It knows its name again.)

The Agreement did not, you are aware, give us all that we wanted, but we had time to frown about that in the future. That moment was for the opening of the prisons and camps, for the return of the guerillas, for the mothers and fathers who saw their sons for the first time in four years, for the sisters who saw their brothers again. Nothing was able to take away from that moment, nothing was able to diminish it, no other thought was able to push it from center stage. You didn't have time to read the Agreement (Ah, yes, there is an agreement). It was a great moment of little moments. The bells sang noisily.

YOU MENTIONED the concentration camps? No door up to this time had ever opened like the doors of the camps. They suddenly widened to almost limitless proportions; they put on their festive dress (two rows of gold medallions around the necks) and opened. They opened as the sky opens to the spring, as the spring opens to the sky. They opened like a blazing August bay opens to a sea breeze or the depth of a ravine opens to the wings of a swallow. They opened wide, from the heart, to the crowd of thousands that waited outside—men, women, and children of all ages (a festival like before, but no longer silent; today it was noisy and boisterous).

A priest came first. His hands were spread to feel the opening of the doors, to explore the entire opening, to judge its width.

And then all the others. They did not walk, they rushed forward as if they were afraid that the door might close again before they had gotten out. They carried their bundles, their luggage, the woodwork they had made during the endless years of imprisonment, the little model caiques (that traveled and carried you far away from the camps), and the icons of the Virgin Mary they had painted. The air was filled with names, voices, cries of joy, and embraces.

Everyone went on to church, to kneel and kiss the marble floor, to light a candle.

FOR YOU who know that Nikos should return on this day, but will not, all these events are another wound, another death. Nikos? Who was Nikos? Mother is alone in the house wandering about. She grips the walls, she fumbles about Nikos's bed, father's desk and armchair, and Stalo's purse and books. Mother does not hear the noise of the crowds, she has no contact with the festivities outside at all. She has no place on this day since no one will knock on the closed doors of the house. The prisons and detention camps will not send anyone home to her, neither father (I haven't told you that he won't be coming back) nor Stalo (I haven't told you that she won't be coming back either).

Unfortunately it is necessary to repeat a foreign saying (there aren't other suitable words). Let her be! Let her be!

And don't tell her that I will not return, don't let her know that I am gone as well. Don't let her grope at my books or my school cap. In her mind, at least let her have me. Let me be with her, let her hold me in her arms, so we can listen to the sound of the bells together. I will trick her into thinking that we are waiting for the others.

"Do you hear, my son?"

"Yes" (that old, drawn out "yes" without vowels, the "yes" of the Christmas bells, the "yes" of the first bombs). "Yes, Mother. They are coming. We are coming."

117

NOTES TO THE TEXT

Words that appear in English in Montis's text are italicized in this translation. The effect of the few English words in the Latin alphabet in a novel written in the Greek alphabet is of course much more striking to the eye than what one sees here.

P. 4. On 21 October 1931, there was a procession of angry Greeks to the Governor's House in Cyprus. After its arrival and some confrontations with police, some of the group attacked the building and set fire to it.

P. 6. These are references to people and incidents from the Greek War of Independence (1821-28). Theodore Kolokotronis, one of the most famous Greek generals, was often depicted wearing his helmet, with a bushy beard and thick eyebrows. Athanasios Dhiakos was impaled and burnt by the Turks in March 1821 near Thermopylae. The Inn of Gravia (May 1821), Missolonghi (March 1826, also famous as the place where Byron died), and Maniaki (May 1825) were battles in which outnumbered Greeks fought valiantly in a losing cause.

P. 7. The Monastery of St. George is near the city of Larnaca. Young women would visit to ask the saint to find them good husbands.

P. 8. The Monastery of Kykko contains one of three icons of the virgin in the Greek world reputed to be painted by the apostle Luke. The other two are in the Monastery of Megaspilion in the northwest corner of the Peloponnesus and on the island of Tinos.

P. 11. This is a reference to statements by Winston Churchill and others that all those who served would share in the rewards of victory, and to the recruiting slogan used in Cyprus, "Fight for Freedom, Fight for Greece." Since Cyprus was a British colony there was no conscription during World War II, but many Cypriots volunteered.

P. 16. EOKA stands for *Ethniki Organosis Kyprion Agoniston* (National Organization of Cypriot Fighters).

Dighenis Akritas is the hero of a Byzantine epic-romance and numerous folk ballads; some of the latter recount his wrestling match with Charon, the mythological ferryman on the River Styx.

P. 22. George Grivas, the leader of EOKA who went by the name of Dighenis, was born in Cyprus and attended the Pan-Cyprian Gymnasium before he went to the Athens Military Academy and began a career in the Greek military. In the 1940s, he started a right wing organization called "X" that had dubious and fascist tendencies, and none of the major Greek political parties would embrace him.

P. 26. There is a legend of a drought that went on for so long that the island was depopulated. It was repopulated only in 337, when St. Helena, mother of the emperor Constantine, arrived in Cyprus with a piece of the true cross, which has been held in the Monastery of Stavrovouni ever since.

P. 37. Gregoris Afxentiou was trapped in a cave by British forces on 3 March 1956. He refused to surrender, and the British could not lure him out or kill him until they poured gasoline into the cave and set it on fire. Kyriakos Matsis was trapped alone in similar circumstance on 11 November 1958, but was killed when grenades were thrown into the cave. Four EOKA fighters were trapped in a barn in Liopetri on 2 September 1958 and killed trying to escape after it was set on fire. The text refers to these incidents several times.

P. 39. Mesaoria is the plain that lies between the Pentadactylos and Troodos mountain ranges.

P. 50. Archbishop Makarios was exiled to the island of Mache in the Seychelles, in the Indian Ocean.

P. 52. Platres is a resort town in the Troodos Mountains where the ravines attract nightingales. The nightingales of Platres became famous in literature from the line in George Seferis's poem "Helen," "The nightingales won't let you sleep in Platres," first published in 1955 (*The Collected Poems of George Seferis*, trans. Edmund Keeley and Philip Sherrard [Princeton University Press, 1967], 345).

P. 53. Michael Karaolis and Andreas Demetriou, the first persons to be executed during the Cyprus Revolt, were hung on 10 May 1956. Their actual ages were twenty-three and twenty-one.

P. 54. The quotations from the "Hymn to Liberty" are from Dionysius Solomos, *Faith and Motherland: Collected Poems*, trans. Marios Byron Raizis (Nostos Books, 1998), 23.

P. 113. Montis either copied or received copies of these letters which were displayed in the National Museum of Ireland in Dublin, but we have not been able to find copies of the original texts in English in a printed source. What we provide is a translation of the Greek in the novel.

Sean MacDiarmada, or Sean McDermott, was one of the leaders of the rebellion against British rule in Dublin on Easter Monday, 1916, and was executed on 12 May. Francis Flood was arrested after the killings of British intelligence officials on 21 November 1920, known as "Bloody Sunday," and executed in March 1921. Tim Pat Coogan commented on the execution of Flood and the others arrested for those killings, "as often happens in such cases none of the accused was in any way involved" (*Michael Collins: A Biography* [London: Hutchinson, 1990], 181).

P. 114. Montis here translates part of the proclamation distributed on Easter Monday, 1916, signed by Sean MacDiarmada and seven others. The original English text is provided here.

P. 119. There is a reference to the holiday called "Ochi" or "No" day, 28 November 1940, when the leader of Greece answered a request for free transit of Axis troops through the country with the single word in Greek, "No."

Books on the Historical Background

Nancy Crawshaw, *The Cyprus Revolt: An Account of the Struggle for Union with Greece* (London: Allen and Unwin, 1978).

Charles Foley, *Island in Revolt* (London: Longmans, 1962).

Robert Holland, *Britain and the Revolt in Cyprus, 1954-1959* (Oxford: Clarendon Press, 1998).

ABOUT THE TRANSLATORS

DAVID ROESSEL teaches Greek language and literature at the Richard Stockton College of New Jersey. He is the author of *In Byron's Shadow: Modern Greece in English and American Literature*, which received the 2001 Modern Language Association Prize for Independent Scholars and the 2002 Elma Dangerfield Award of the International Byron Society. He has lived in both Nicosia and Athens.

SOTERIOS G. STAVROU was born in Cyprus and educated in the United States in English literature at Augsburg College and in ancient history and the classics at the University of Minnesota. His translations of Greek literature into English include *The Free Spirit* by George Theotokas and (with Donald E. Martin) *Tetralogy of the Times* by G. Philippou Pierides.

NOSTOS BOOKS ON
MODERN GREEK HISTORY AND CULTURE

Theofanis G. Stavrou, *general editor*
University of Minnesota

1. Yannis Ritsos, *Eighteen Short Songs of the Bitter Motherland*. Translated from Greek by Amy Mims with illustrations by the poet. Edited with an introduction by Theofanis G. Stavrou. 1974.
2. Kimon Friar, *The Spiritual Odyssey of Nikos Kazantzakis*. Edited with an introduction by Theofanis G. Stavrou. 1979.
3. Kostas Kindinis, *Poems: Reinvestigations and Descent from the Cross*. Translated from Modern Greek with a preface by Kimon Friar. 1980.
4. Andonis Decavalles, *Pandelis Prevelakis and the Value of a Heritage*. Including *Rethymno as a Style of Life*, by Pandelis Prevelakis, translated from Greek by Jean H. Woodhead. Edited with an introduction by Theofanis G. Stavrou. 1981.
5. John Anton, *Critical Humanism as a Philosophy of Culture: The Case of E. P. Papanoutsos*. Edited with an introduction by Theofanis G. Stavrou. 1981.
6. Ioanna Tsatsos, *My Brother George Seferis*. Translated from Greek by Jean Demos with a preface by Eugene Current-Garcia. 1982.
7. Donald C. Swanson, *Vocabulary of Modern Spoken Greek (English-Greek and Greek-English)*. With the assistance of Sophia P. Djaferis and a foreword by Theofanis G. Stavrou. 1982.
8. Nikos Kazantzakis, *Two Plays: Sodom and Gomorrah and Comedy: A Tragedy in One Act*. Translated from Greek with an introduction to *Sodom and Gomorrah* by Kimon Friar. Including an introduction to *Comedy: A Tragedy in One Act* by Karl Kerényi, translated by Peter Bien. 1982.
9. George Thaniel, *Homage to Byzantium: The Life and Work of Nikos Gabriel Pentzikis*. 1983.
10. Theofanis G. Stavrou, *Angelos Sikelianos and the Delphic Idea*. Including *Life with Angelos Sikelianos*, by Anna Sikelianos, and *Sibyl*, by Angelos Sikelianos. Forthcoming.
11. Theofanis G. Stavrou and Constantine Trypanis, *Kostis Palamas: A Portrait and an Appreciation*. Including *Iambs and Anapaests* and *Ascraeus*, by Kostis Palamas. 1985.
12. Ioanna Tsatsos, *Poems*. Translated from Greek by Jean Demos with an introduction by C. A. Trypanis. 1984.

13. George Theotokas, *Leonis: A Novel*. Translated from Greek by Donald E. Martin. 1985.
14. Petros Haris, *The Longest Night: Chronicle of a Dead City*. Translated from Greek by Theodore Sampson. 1985.
15. Louis Coutelle, Theofanis G. Stavrou, and David R. Weinberg, *A Greek Diptych: Dionysios Solomos and Alexandros Papadiamantis*. 1986.
16. Yannis Ritsos, *Monovasia and The Women of Monemvasia*. Translated from Modern Greek with an introduction by Kimon Friar and Kostas Myrsiades. 1987.
17. Takis Papatsonis, *Ursa Minor and Other Poems*. Translated from Modern Greek with an introduction by Kimon Friar and Kostas Myrsiades. 1988.
18. Pandelis Prevelakis, *The Cretan: A Trilogy in One Volume*. Translated from Modern Greek by Abbott Rick and Peter Mackridge, with an introduction by Peter Mackridge. 1991.
19. Nikiforos Vrettakos, *Gifts in Abeyance: Last Poems, 1981-91*. Translated from Modern Greek with an introduction by David Connolly. 1992.
20. Kiki Dimoula. *Lethe's Adolescence*. Translated from Modern Greek with an introduction by David Connolly. 1996.
21. G. Philippou Pierides, *Tetralogy of the Times: Stories of Cyprus*. Translated from Greek by Donald E. Martin and Soterios G. Stavrou, with a preface by Theofanis G. Stavrou. 1998.
22. Dionysios Solomos, *Faith and Motherland: Collected Poems*. Translated from Greek with annotations and an introduction by Marios Byron Raizis. 1998.
23. Costas Montis, *Closed Doors: An Answer to Bitter Lemons by Lawrence Durrell*. Translated from Greek by David Roessel and Soterios G. Stavrou, with an introduction by David Roessel. 2004.